SHADOW OF THE ROSE

The Esoterism of the Romantic Tradition

Charles Upton
Jennifer Doane Upton

SHADOW
OF THE ROSE

The Esoterism of the
Romantic Tradition

O Rose, thou art sick.
The invisible worm
That flies in the night
In the howling storm:

Has found out thy bed
Of crimson joy,
And his dark secret love
Does thy life destroy.

William Blake,
'The Sick Rose'

SOPHIA PERENNIS

SAN RAFAEL, CA

First published in the USA
by Sophia Perennis
© Charles and Jennifer Doane Upton 2008

Series editor: James R. Wetmore

For information, address:
Sophia Perennis, P.O. Box 151011
San Rafael, CA 94915
sophiaperennis.com

Library of Congress Cataloging-in-Publication Data

Upton, Charles, 1948–
Shadow of the rose: the esoterism of the Romantic tradition/
Charles Upton and Jennifer Doane Upton.

p. cm.

ISBN 978-1-59731-079-6 (pbk: alk. paper)
1. Love—Religious aspects. 2. Love. 3. Nostalgia.
I. Upton, Jennifer Doane. II. Title
BL 626.4.U68   2008
306.701—dc22   2008003159

CONTENTS

Introduction

Human love has fallen on hard times; it has been 'officially discredited'. Even liberal humanitarianism is not what it used to be; how then can romantic love, which in its origins is essentially aristocratic (in Meister Eckhart's sense when he said 'the soul is an aristocrat') find any place in today's world? The truth is, it cannot. The world is too small for it. The place of romantic love is nowhere in this world; its place is in the human soul, whose own proper place is in the eternal self-knowledge of God.

The word 'romance' has to do with the nostalgia of medieval Europe for the imperial greatness of former times, for the 'grandeur that was Rome'. Only the traditional sense of historical time as a progressive descent could have cast as 'romantic' those cynical, canny, hard-nosed practitioners of *realpolitik*, the Romans of the imperial era. What the medieval romancers could not see, apparently, is that romantic love, though opposed in many ways to Papal Rome and the ethos (or at least the posture) of the official church, was essentially Christian. If Jesus Christ had not championed the cause of particular men and women—a despised Samaritan woman, a Pharisee, a Roman centurion, a hated tax collector, a madman, a prostitute—against a sacred law grown petrified, punctilious and inhuman, according to which man was made for the Sabbath not the Sabbath for man, romance would never have been born in the western world. Speaking in alchemical terms, the Sulfur of romance, its masculine pole, was an Arabo-Persian tradition of narrative and lyric poetry on romantic themes, much of it filled with Sufi spiritual allegory; the Mercury of it, the feminine pole, was the mass of Celtic material bequeathed to Europe as a whole by Britain and Brittany and Ireland; but the vessel in which these two elements met and married, the Salt of it, was medieval Christendom. The bride was the archaic Goddess of the Celtic twilight;

the groom was chivalrous and militant Islam, the latest and last of the great revelations; the officiating priest, who pronounced them man and wife, was Jesus Christ. If Christianity built a whole ethical culture on the mystery that 'whatsoever ye do to the least of these, my brethren, ye do unto Me,' and a rich mystical tradition on 'He who has seen Me has seen the Father,' romantic love echoed the Christian revelation in a different mode by unveiling a closely allied secret: that, in the words of Ibn al-'Arabi, 'He who has seen a beautiful woman has seen God.'

According to René Guénon, romance is to be classed among the lesser, feminine mysteries, and is the particular province—speaking in Hindu terms—of the *kshatriya* or warrior caste, just as the greater mysteries, those having to do with the realization of God and Liberation from the world of name and form, are the province of the *brahmins*, the priests. And certainly the love-and-war mythology of chivalric romance was developed by the European equivalent of the *kshatriyas*, the royalty and the nobility, partly in opposition to sacerdotal authority—an authority that was violently re-asserted against it by the Albigensian Crusade, the only Western Christian crusade mounted against an entirely European enemy.

The lesser mysteries are essentially psychic rather than pneumatic; they have to do with character development, with the achievement of psycho-physical balance, with the full attainment of the human form—a state the alchemists symbolized by the Philosopher's Stone and the Alchemical Gold. Only a fully alchemized soul can embark on the path of the greater Spiritual mysteries without suffering damage in the presence of the tremendous Majesty of God, or being led into delusion and dissipation by Her ravishing Beauty.

Yet the Spiritual mysteries also have their 'romantic' element, without which there would be no such thing as Tantra in the Hindu universe. The reflection of the Majesty and Beauty of God in a beloved human being, and the inner psychic encounter with one's contra-sexual archetype (in Jungian terms, with *anima* or *animus*)—both of which are necessary for the completion of the lesser mysteries—are limited reflections of the eternal polarity between the Divine as Absolute Witness, *Atman* or *Shiva*, and the Divine as universal manifestation *in divinis, Maya* or *Shakti*—a polarity that nonetheless, in essence, is 'not two' (*advaita*). In Judaism, this polarity appears as the relationship between Yah-weh and His *shekhina*, His outward and visible manifestation conceived in feminine terms, or between Him and the figure of Holy Wisdom in the 8th and 9th chapters of Proverbs. As for Islam, the polarity of the Divine Essence, *al-Dhat* (a feminine noun) and the synthesis of all the Names of God, *Allah* (an essentially masculine figure, Who is nonetheless beyond all sexual polarity), is embraced and resolved in the Reality of the One. In Christianity, the primal polarity appears as the Virgin and the Child Jesus, where Jesus is in one sense the Formless Absolute ('I and the Father are one') and the Virgin the matrix of universal manifestation ('my soul doth magnify the Lord'), while in another sense He is the quintessential Form or *icon* of God emerging from the Black Virgin, the Theotokos as symbol of the Essence and vessel of the Holy Spirit, that aspect of God which transcends all polarities, even the primal polarity of the Father and the Son. And in heterodox Christian Gnosticism, particularly in *The Gospel of Philip*, the Tantric polarity appears as the supposed love relationship between Jesus and Mary Magdalene.

Romance is the worship of the Formless by means of form. The Beloved must take concrete form in our lives so as to draw us beyond form entirely; He must become as we are so that we may become as He is. But as soon as the Formless Absolute is identified with any form whatsoever, *Maya* is born—and *Maya*, according to the Hindus, has two faces: *avidya-maya*, the magical apparition of God as the universe, which ultimately veils Him, and *vidya-maya*, the magical apparition of God apparently within the universe, designed to lead the soul beyond the formal universe entirely—including the Form of God Himself.

Romantic love is the province of *vidya-maya*, best represented in the western tradition by the figure of Beatrice from the *Divine Comedy* of Dante Aligheri. *Avida-maya*, for Dante, is represented in one of his poems by the stony-hearted woman Pietra—

symbol of the World, or the worldly Church—but Beatrice is the type of Holy Wisdom, the *vidya-maya* that led the poet not into final, literal union with her, but beyond form entirely (including her own) in the last cantos of the *Paradiso*. *Vidya-maya* and *avidya-maya* also appear in the Book of Proverbs, in the guise of two prostitutes, the one named 'Wisdom' and the other the 'foolish woman'. Both stand on the high places of the city and call out to foolish men—as prostitutes will—but Wisdom calls fools only to invite them to realize Wisdom itself, while the foolish woman calls them to live out their foolishness on its own level, thereby leading them to inevitable destruction. (The Jews did not practice sacred prostitution, but they were surrounded by cultures that did; in the 8th and 9th chapters of Proverbs, that institution is both spiritually sublimated and brilliantly satirized—a wonderful example of the metaphysical wit and irony that fills the Old Testament, and the Gospels too, which is so rarely seen for what it is.)

So the figure of the Beloved in romantic love is a manifestation of *vidya-maya*. But *Maya* does not come neatly divided into *vidya* and *avidya*; She would not be *Maya* if She did. The division between them is in 'the eye of the beholder'. The spiritual Heart, open to the influx of God's Wisdom, sees the world as a theophany, as *vidya-maya*. The ego (what the Sufis call the *nafs al-ammara*, the 'soul commanding to evil') sees the world as an opaque, literal object with nothing behind it, this being *avidya-maya* precisely. And here we have the crux, the *agon*, of romantic love: will the lover treat his Beloved as an object of his ego, thereby betraying Love, or will he recognize her as a manifestation of Love Itself, and so remain faithful to his god *Amor*?

The battle that is inseparable from the way of romantic love is always that between the ego and the spiritual Heart; whatever earthly struggles the lover must engage in are nothing but outer-world projections of this primal choice. The same parting of the ways is represented in the story of the advent of White Buffalo Cow Woman, the 'prophetess' who brought the sacred pipe to the Lakota (the closest equivalent of which, in Old World tradition, is probably the Hebrew Ark of the Covenant).

When she appeared naked on the prairie before two Lakota braves, one of them wanted to rape her, while the other recognized her as holy, numinous, *wakan*. A cloud descended over the lustful brave, inside of which could be heard the sound of snakes hissing and striking; and when the cloud lifted, there was nothing left of him but a naked skeleton. White Buffalo Cow Woman then turned to the other brave, and told him to announce her coming.

So the way of romance is essentially that of the transformation of lust into true love—not by the 'right-hand path' of asceticism and renunciation, but by the 'left-hand path' of loyalty-in-erotic-fascination, of faithfulness to form in the very process of transcending form. It is by this struggle with desire on the field of desire itself that the soul rises out of the sub-human instinctiveness of the natural order and attains to the 'Human Form Divine'. (When Lucius Apuleius, in the myth of Amor and Psyche recounted in his novel *The Golden Ass*, shows Psyche—the human soul—as struggling free from the power of Aphrodite in order to be united with her lover Amor, or Eros—Aphrodite's son—he is telling the same story.)

But a final question remains: Is one's human beloved a 'mere' symbol of the Divine, a simple means to an End? The Sufis call human love 'figurative love', reserving the term 'true love' only for the One Beloved. In the words of the Hindu sage Yajnavalkya: 'Truly, not for the sake of the husband is the husband dear, but a husband is dear for the sake of the Self. Truly, not for the sake of the wife is the wife dear, but a wife is dear for the sake of the Self.' And while this is entirely true—profoundly so, in fact—in actual human situations a glib recitation of this and similar teachings is sometimes in danger of introducing an element of crassness, by which the human beloved is *slighted* in the name of the Love of God. But to do this is to slight God too; since God is the Essence of forms, not simply that which is realized when forms are transcended—since He is Immanence as well as Transcendence—love for the human beloved may also be seen as an actual example of true love, in the recognition that she is not only a veil that hides the True Beloved—though she certainly is that—but also a living *instance* of that Beloved, of God's saving Mercy, in space and time: limited and temporary, but nonetheless real—which is to say: limited and temporary, but nonetheless eternal. If Beatrice had been for Dante *nothing but* a symbol of Holy Wisdom, there would have been no *Divine Comedy*. She also had to be a human woman, with human limitations, whom Dante truly loved, through he only saw her a few times in this life. In the Way of Romantic Love, the Beloved, if she is to save us, must be both truly human and truly divine, as Christ is—as we all are, in essence, if the truth be known. How else could we be 'co-heirs with Christ' and 'all gods, and sons of the Most High'? In Christian terms, the difference between us and Christ is that He both knows this and is this from all Eternity, while we can only know and be what He is by the free gift His atonement and His grace—and the ultimate sacrifice required of every one of us, if we are to receive it.

As a civilization, we have forgotten the metaphysical depths of romantic love. First we sentimentalized it in order to make it available to all, including those whose understanding was limited to the sentimental level, because the inherent generosity of love demanded it. But in that reckless generosity we lost the *exclusivity* of love, the loyalty to the One and Only—after which the sentimentality into which love had fallen became the breach in the wall of love's citadel through which the world could slander, satirize, debunk and ultimately destroy it. And it is in the ruins of love's citadel that we presently live, like barbarians huddled in the ruins of Rome or Babylon, wondering what purpose these ancient works might once have served for our ancestors, and telling each other that human beings could not have built them, only the giants or the *jinn*. And it is true that no human being could have built them, but God alone.

The purpose of this book is that romantic love be 'remembered'—as Isis *re-membered* Osiris when she went in search his scattered limbs, gathered them together, and brought him back to life again by the power of her divine breath, and her human kiss. No matter how hidden it may become, the 'chain-of-transmission' of the spiritual romantics is never broken, because it is a reflection of an eternal face of Humanity. Some few in every generation wake up one day to find themselves accepted companions of the Fedeli d'Amore, the faithful-to-Love. But only if the tradition of spiritual love is consciously remembered can they realize what has happened to them, begin to collect their scattered history, and remember their pre-eternal vow to meet—however briefly, and no matter what the cost—in this world.

PART ONE:
THE OUTWARD DIMENSION

by Charles Upton

To my wife Jenny
I dedicate this short passage
from our long conversation

Love in the Kali-Yuga

I

My basic intellectual world-view, for the past twenty years, has been founded largely on the works of the writers of the Traditionalist School—René Guénon, Ananda Coomaraswamy, Frithjof Schuon, Titus Burckhardt, Martin Lings, Seyyed Hossein Nasr, James Cutsinger, Reza Shah-Kazemi, and many others—who have resurrected and articulated universal metaphysical principles in a way that is unique in our time, and rare in any time. Given the exalted nature of their standpoint, and the prevailing spiritual darkness, their teachings will necessarily appeal only to a few. And it should be obvious that the power of these teachings to extend themselves into areas ruled by contemporary beliefs and assumptions will be strictly limited. Nonetheless, the border between traditional principles and those realms that will never glimpse the light of them has yet to be fully surveyed for our present historical moment.

The Traditionalists, however, also appear to have been affected to a degree by the *shadow* of universal metaphysics: namely, the inability to see, understand, and take into account the uniqueness of human personalities—the rights, dangers, qualities and dynamics, as well as the metaphysical meaning, of the *particular case*. And one consequence of this lack is that they have had little to say on a certain spiritual 'tradition' that is integral to western civilization, the only one that treated the uniqueness of the human personality *metaphysically*, the only one that viewed that personality *sub specie aeternitatis*: the tradition of romantic love.

The culture of Romance that flourished in the 12th century Provence of the troubadours has many tributaries and ramifications. Romance, at least as a literary genre, was essentially a synthesis of Celtic lore and various Arabo-Persian influences, but it was one that, for all its heterodox tendencies (expressed theologically in terms of the Albigensian heresy), could only have been accomplished within the hermetic vessel of medieval Christian culture. Without the doctrine of the Incarnation, the primacy of human love for a particular human beloved would never have remained allegorical; it would never have been born.

In its widest reach, romantic love must be seen as related to ancient European material such as the Tristan and Isolde legend, to Arabic love-legends and their Persian renditions, like Nizami's *Layla and Majnun* and *Khosrau and Shirin*, and Jami's re-telling of the Biblical and Qur'anic story of Joseph and Potiphar's wife, *Yusuf and Zuleikha*. The Song of Solomon from the Old Testament is part of it, as well as *The Golden Ass* of Lucius Apuleius and, much later, the *The Tale of Genji* by Lady Murasaki. The poetry of Hafiz and Rumi is central to it within Islam, only to be equaled by *The Interpreter of Ardent Desires* of Ibn al-'Arabi. The Sahaja poetry of the popular Vaishnava poets of Bengal, such as Chandidas, Vidyapati and Kalidasa, is a branch of it, as well as the poetry composed in honor of Shiva and His Shakti, and the devotional verse of Kabir, Rabi'a and Mirabai; so too is the *udhri* poetry of early Muslim Arabia, which is perhaps the true ancestor of the troubadour poetry of Muslim Spain, though it predated that movement by half a millennium. Through the grail romances, it is related both to Celtic legend and the whole world of western chivalry. Wolfram Von Eschenbach's *Parzival*, in particular, connects it with both the alchemical tradition and the Knights Templars. In many ways it reached its highest devel-opment in the works of Dante Alighieri, who was deeply influ-enced by the troubadour tradition (especially the works of Arnaut Daniel), and incorporated into his *Commedia* and *Vita Nuova* many of the doctrines of the Fedeli d'Amore, the 'Faithful to Love', that loose association of fellow-poets and/or initiatic secret society that has been the subject of so many fascinating speculations by historians of the esoteric. (The Fedeli d'Amore, also known as the Fede Santa, might have been a kind of third order of the Knights Templars, and might also have had certain

Sufi affiliations.) Shakespeare, and other Elizabethan poets, are pregnant with it. Its most explicit if not its deepest cultural expression was through the Courts of Love established by Eleanor of Aquitaine and her daughter, Marie de Champagne.

In the 20th century, under the influence of figures like Ezra Pound, romantic love often became identified with Neo-Pagan historical speculations of an overtly anti-Christian cast. And while it is true that the courtly love culture of southern France had at least a loose cultural affinity with heretical movements such as Catharism (Albigensianism), it is equally true that it functioned as a vital element of the medieval Christian cultural milieu. Likewise the Sahaja poets of India, influenced as they were by the love poetry, Sufi or otherwise, of the Moghuls, which was ultimately Persian in origin, were considered to be heterodox in the eyes of some Hindu authorities—yet what could be more quintessentially Hindu than the Krishna-centered *bhakti* they express? The erotic poetry of Hafiz was frowned upon by the Muslim *ulema*—but if Sufism is the heart of Islam, then Hafiz will always be close to that heart.

It is clear that the romantic love tradition is related both to a powerful strand of *bhaktic* spirituality common to Christianity, Islam and Hinduism, as well as to various initiatory lineages of a more esoteric and *jñanic* nature, such as the Fedeli d'Amore and various Sufi *tariqas*, as revealed in the writings of René Guénon, Titus Burckhardt, Henry Corbin and others. The famous Sufi Ruzbehan Baqli, for example, is often classed as among the 'Fedeli d'Amore' of Islam. But if the Fedeli d'Amore and other esoteric groups dedicated to the practice of romantic love are no longer in force as viable spiritual lineages, some might claim that a too-serious (or too *literal*) interest in the romantic love tradition might distract one from a quest from those esoteric spiritualities that are still operative and effective. Western Romance might justify a literary or antiquarian interest; it might teach us something about the history of western esoterism, but certain it has little substantive to say to us now, in terms of our concrete lives, at the beginning of the third millennium. It is quaint and touching, lit by a delicate nostalgia to the eyes of those susceptible to its charms, but it is certainly not 'the one thing needful'.

On the other hand, just what was that 'one thing needful', according to the Gospels? It was, precisely, the contemplation of God, on the part of a 'romantic' and 'impractical' woman, in the human person of her Beloved [Luke 10:39–42]. As Frithjof Schuon has written, in *Understanding Islam*, 'the "romantic" worlds are precisely those in which God is still probable.'

So why have I taken it upon myself to propose a new look at the tradition of romantic love? Perhaps I was influenced by the discovery that, if the history of my mother's family compiled by my great aunt is accurate, I am 29th in direct (though often female) line from Eleanor of Aquitaine, and thus 31st in line from Guillem de Poitiers, the first troubadour, who came by that distinction in the following way: In one of the many feudal skirmishes of the time, Guillem's father won from a Spanish emir a troupe of singing-girls, who would have known, between them, hundreds of songs at the very least, perhaps thousands. Guillem grew up in a palace surrounded by these women; in effect, they were his nannies. This, undoubtedly, is the precise link between the poetry of the troubadours and the Arabo-Persian tradition, filled with Sufi lore, that it so closely resembles. Of course the influence of values realized by one's ancestors is practically nil, and can even be destructive—a haunting, accusative ghost—unless drawn upon to serve values one is striving to realize in the present moment, in line with God's will; as my great-grandfather used to say: 'Don't be like a potato—the best part of you under ground.' But, family traditions apart, the central reason for my interest is that the pattern of my life has made it necessary for me to speak up against the plague of emotional coldness, psychic numbness, and 'hardness of heart' that is an inescapable part of these 'latter days'.

In II Timothy 3:3, St. Paul says that, as the age draws toward its close, 'natural affection' shall fail. And contemporary American culture—to limit my critique to what I know first hand—shows every evidence of this. For parents to abuse children is common, and it is not unknown for children to murder parents. And the present content and pace of the mass media seem specifically designed to produce a generation of sociopaths, sociopaths affected with attention deficit disorder as well. Bloody violence aside, dialogue on many television dramas has degenerated into an unrelieved stream of threat, abuse and insult, with vicious satire as the only 'comic relief'; products are sold by associating them with the power to hurt other people's feelings; even the dead are subject to abuse and scorn as the 'ultimate losers'. An all-pervasive lovelessness has led to a general emotional flattening and weakening of the texture of the soul, manifesting in gross terms as a plague of psychotic violence, and in a more subtle way as a pandemic lack of what used to be called 'common' courtesy. Nor are these two poles unrelated, since a collective lack of sensitivity to the feelings of others means that everyone is always being offended, and offended people are always getting angry. If it weren't for the fact that our high schools are graduating people who can't read, I would be tempted to propose a kind of 'finishing school' for the general population, where people would be taught such arcane mysteries as 'if someone you consider a friend phones you a number of times but you never return his or her calls, he or she may feel offended', or 'if you (as a man) insult a man's wife in his presence, he may not accept this as a gesture of good will, demonstrating your support for him in the battle of the sexes, but may actually feel insulted himself,' or 'if a man lets you (a woman) know, in a sensitive and respectful way, that he finds you attractive, he has not insulted or harassed or attempted to rape you, but has in fact complimented you.'

Simply stated, a general level of humaneness or common decency can no longer be taken for granted in any social class or sector, and this certainly includes the sector of religious organizations, spiritual groups, and even traditional initiatory paths. In the case of spiritualities that have come to the West from more traditional cultures, where the Hindu caste system or the *shari'ah* of Islam still culturally, if not legally, enforces a set of common norms of interpersonal behavior (norms not necessarily ideal from the western standpoint), the lack of such norms in the West is not always recognized by the exemplars of such spiritualities, nor the full consequences of this cultural vacuum understood. Nor have we who have grown up in the West necessarily come fully to terms with the fact that the common bourgeois decency—however hypocritical it may have been—of our parents' or grandparents' generation (I speak as a member of the Baby Boom) is a thing of the past.

It might be objected that it is not the business of spiritual teachers and the masters of esoteric lineages to teach American adults their table-manners. But it should nonetheless be remembered that, at least insofar as Sufism (my own spiritual path) is concerned, the refinement of the outer personality in human relations is considered integral to spiritual etiquette or *adab*, and that the word *adab* means, in its most literal sense, precisely 'table-manners'.

The *adab* of the Sufi circle, however, is not necessarily applicable, except in spirit, to other areas of interpersonal relations. In a normal, traditional society, or even a bourgeois western one, various areas of life have their own inherent shapeliness, however much or little we may like this or that particular shape. Traditionally speaking there is the world of the family, the world of the 'marketplace', the world of the craft-guild, which in its widest definition would include the 'crafts' of scholarship and war, the world of the academy, and the world of the church or temple or mosque; each of worlds used to have its own particular norms of human relatedness, its own *adab*. Similarly, the traditional Chinese gentleman would possess a set of seals, made of brass or ivory or jade, by which he would sign various documents or art-works; one seal would be reserved for business matters, another for art, a third for matters of love, etc. And in traditional societies, different costumes would be worn for different activities—as we in the West used to wear street clothes, business clothes, work clothes, church clothes, academic robes, 'lounging' clothes (like the smoking-jacket), evening clothes etc., depending on the occasion. We all had a set of formal social 'roles', and we dressed the part. Now, however, it is common for one's church, or corporation, or army, to claim that 'we are your family'; the crucial borders between these different sectors of life—like the biological borders between discrete eco-systems— have broken down, with the result that corporations may now act like churches, or families be run like armies. And apart from the bride's dress and veil, the tuxedo, the military uniform, and certain quaint holdovers like the chef's cap and the mortar- board, it seems we all dress in shorts or blue jeans now; I even saw people in 'designer' blue jeans at the San Francisco Opera. Priests still wear vestments, at least on occasion, but the nun's habit has almost entirely disappeared.

In traditional societies, however, virtually everyone, or at least every man, participated in a set of discrete social worlds; and so, when someone felt called to approach a realm that was not com- mon to all, such as the royal court, the contemplative order (in Christianity) or the Sufi *tariqa* (in Islam), the guardians of these realms could be much more certain than their present-day counterparts that the petitioner was not seeking admittance because he or she was searching for a substitute family, or trying to overcome a sense of alienation felt at work, or trying to live out an unclear or unfulfilled call to the life of the scholar or the warrior, or attempting to establish a rudimentary faith in God. All these needs were largely taken care of, to one degree or another, by the greater society—which meant that, in the case of a call to the contemplative life within Christianity, to Sufism within Islam, or to the life of a *sanyasin* within Hinduism, the one renouncing 'the world' knew exactly what was being renounced. The 'technical' name for this state of affairs was *civilization*.

This is not the case, however, in present American society, nor in many other contemporary societies the world over. Affil- iation with a church is no longer taken for granted. Work is no longer based on initiation and craft competence, or family tradi- tion. And community as a network of interrelated families is falling apart, just as the family itself is dissolving. Civilization has broken down. Consequently, many who are attracted to a spiri- tual path may half-consciously be seeking a family, or a guild, or an exoteric religious organization, or the father they never knew—even if, on another level, their call to the esoteric path is essentially valid. This is why I believe it is necessary for those of us dedicated to traditional esoterism to address ourselves more fully to the question of the role humane interpersonal relations should play in the spiritual life—to *love* in the widest as well as the deepest sense of that term.

II

Human love, whether or not it is directly and consciously inspired by Divine love (as all love is, indirectly at least), can be divided into three channels: Agape, Eros and Amor. In defining these terms I am following the lead of Joseph's Campbell who, in his *Creative Mythology*, distinguishes between an impersonal, orgiastic Eros and a personal, properly 'romantic' Amor. Although the word 'Eros' is often used—by C.S. Lewis, for example—to cover both types of love (*amor*, after all, is the Latin word used to translate the Greek *eros*), as well as to denote love in its most universal and transpersonal expressions (cf. the Sufi use of *Ishk*, the closest synonym for Eros in Arabic, to denote passionate love for God), the distinction Campbell draws is central to my argument. And so, recognizing that the division is imperfect, I'll define the three as follows:

Agape is charitable love, what is usually called 'Christian' love. It is related more to groups than to individuals; it is impersonal, generous, detached, and motivated by the need of the recipient. Eros is love as defined by the universe of desire, hence sexual love is its most intense expression on the human plane. It is more related to individuals than to groups, though it has a group expression as well, i.e. an orgiastic aspect; it is impersonal, demanding, often attached, and motivated by the need of the giver. Agape stretches from the coolly professional love of the physician or social worker at its lowest extreme, through the love shared by a community or fellowship of believers, to a spiritually-motivated charity that worships God by serving That One in everyone, including the poor, the sick and the destitute, according to Christ's words: 'Whatsoever ye do unto the least of these, my brethren, ye do unto Me.' Its best-known contemporary exemplar is Mother Theresa. Eros stretches from brutal lust at its lowest extreme, through the passionate love of nature and the mutually-delightful sharing of pleasure between lovers, to the self-annihilating love of God as expressed in the *bhaktic* ecstasy. Like Agape, however, Eros has an impersonal quality; the human beloved is loved more as a physical or psychological type than as a complete person. And in the ecstasy of *bhaktic* union, the personhood of both the devotee and his Deity are swept away. Agape is indiscriminate in terms of its object, while Eros is indiscriminate in terms of its expression. But Amor is discrimination incarnate. Not only is Amor directed toward a unique human object, or toward God not as the Universal Reality but as the Unique One—it is also uniquely sensitive to the *boundary* between lover and Beloved. Agape loves just anyone, and is cultivated toward that end. Eros loves with passionate abandon, in the absence of which it is only a pale reflection of its true self. But Amor bases its decision whether to hide or express itself on the willingness of its object to receive that expression. Thus it alone of the three types of love is intimately bound up with courtesy, the virtue that is most closely related to the recognition of boundaries and limits, and most sensitive to the specific emotional quality of the moment. It is thus the most personal of the three. When the Prophet Muhammad, peace and blessing be upon him, during his ascension from the Temple Mount in Jerusalem to the celestial worlds, encountered that revelation of God designated in the Qur'an as *the lote-tree of the furthest limit*, he attained perhaps his greatest intimacy with God, in view of which it is permissible to speculate that he may have been seized by Divine Eros, or *Ishk*. But then his vision of God came to an end; it was once again veiled. It was precisely at this point that Eros would have been transformed into Amor. The Qur'an (53:16–18, Pickthall translation) says of this event: *When that which shroudeth did enshroud the lote tree, the eye turned not aside nor yet was overbold.* The *lote tree* perhaps represents the limit of what can be known about God. When his overpowering vision of God was hidden, the Prophet's attention *turned not aside nor yet was overbold*; he was neither indifferent nor curious; he neither became distracted, nor did he seek to pry into the

Divine Mysteries. Here we see the root of courtesy in the human relationship to God. When one is in the presence of one's Beloved, and She in a reticent mood, it is impolite to boldly stare, and equally impolite to let one's attention wander—or to sulk, or to fawn, or to make demands. The practice is simply to wait, in humility, in vigilance, in self-respect, upon Her good pleasure.

As for Agape, Frithjof Schuon, in *Spiritual Perspectives and Human Facts,* pairs it with the virtue of humility:

> Humility means to look on oneself in the limiting state of individuation; it means to gaze on the ego, on limitation and nothingness. Charity means looking around one; it means seeing God in one's neighbor, and also seeing oneself there, but this time not as pure limitation, but as a creature of God and made in His image.

In other words, self-involvement, when seen as it really is, is abasement, while relatedness, when seen in its true light, is as aspect of the Mercy of God. Only the one who can see himself objectively can know his own ego as a humiliating limitation, and only the *gnostic*—who sees, as it were, with the eye of God—can be perfectly objective. It is this very *jñanic* objectivity that liberates human love from the limitations of the subjective dimension, with its inevitable ignorance and selfishness, and allows affection and relatedness to come to their full flower in the objective light of God.

It is culturally easy for us to see charitable love as an aspect of spirituality, and culturally possible to see the spiritual face of Eros. But the spirituality of personal or romantic love—Amor—is deeply veiled. The 'world', the web of collective egotism, is profoundly threatened by it, which is why it takes every opportunity to slander and destroy it. From one point of view, Amor could be defined as a synthesis between Eros and Agape, with Eros functioning as the emotional and sexual energy of Amor, and Agape as its aspect of compassion and willing self-sacrifice. So a contemplatively sublimated Eros is a necessary part of romantic love. But the *regime* of Eros, of impersonal and/or instinctive attraction, often appears as Amor's enemy. Just as the 'commanding *nafs*', the lower or passional soul in Sufi terminology, actively opposes the realization of the Spirit and the development of spiritual love, so the regime of impersonal attraction I am here calling 'erotic' deliberately scorns and sabotages the personal or romantic kind of love, Amor.

The story of this conflict is told in the famous tale of 'Amor and Psyche' which appears in *The Golden Ass* of Lucius Apuleius. Psyche is a girl who is so beautiful that the people begin to neglect the service of the love goddess Aphrodite, and worship her instead. Personal love, in other words, is beginning to take the place of impersonal Eros. This, of course, angers the Goddess, who sends her son Amor (Eros in Greek, who is more familiar to us as Cupid) to punish Psyche for her transgressions by making her fall in love with the most wretched and unworthy of lovers—which turns out, ironically, to be Amor himself. (It is interesting that the Goddess of Love can lay no greater curse upon Psyche than Love itself, which already implies a subtle indictment of the regime of impersonal Eros the Goddess represents.)

Meanwhile Psyche's father receives an oracle from Apollo which commands that Psyche be married to a monstrous dragon. She is left alone on a crag at the mercy of the beast, but is carried by the wind to a magic palace where she makes passionate love to him, but only in the dark; she is never allowed to see him. Next Psyche's sisters appear and convince her, out of jealousy, that her new husband is a horrible monster. They prevail upon her to shine the light of a lamp upon him, thus breaking the taboo that holds their marriage together, and then kill him with a knife. But as she approaches his sleeping figure with the lamp, she sees that she is married not to a monster but to the God of Love himself. Then she 'accidentally' pricks herself on the head of one of his arrows, and so falls hopelessly in love with him—in the full light of knowledge this time, not merely in the darkness of blind passion. Then a drop of hot oil falls upon him from the lamp, and burns him; he awakens and flies away, abandoning her. But the drop of oil has had the same effect on him as his arrow has had on Psyche. Now Love himself is in love, consequently the hatred and jealousy of Aphrodite falls upon him as well. The Goddess, his mother, imprisons him.

Aphrodite captures Psyche as well, and tortures her. Then she sets her a series of difficult and dangerous tasks, in hopes of ending her life. She must sort a mass of mixed seeds, but is helped by the ants. She must gather the golden fleece of the wild Sun Rams, but succeeds through the advice of a talking reed. She must obtain some of the deadly water of the river Styx, but is aided by the eagle of Zeus. Finally, she is required to descend to the underworld and bring up for Aphrodite a box of Persephone's beauty cream, which she is forbidden to open. Psyche succeeds in the task, but breaks the taboo, opens the box, spreads the beauty cream destined for the Goddess on her own human face, and falls into a magic sleep. Is seems as if all her struggles have been in vain. But while carrying out her tasks, Psyche has constantly been searching for Amor, her beloved— and so now, at the last moment, Amor arrives to rescue her. He pricks Psyche with one of his arrows, and she awakes. Amor then takes her away to Olympus, the abode of the gods, where he marries her, and by so doing makes Psyche an immortal goddess.

Aphrodite's jealousy of Psyche is the resistance of the regime of impersonal Eros to the development of full personal love, which is shown not simply as a path of devotion to the god Amor, but one of *apotheosis*—complete spiritual realization. But the tasks imposed by Aphrodite are not just arbitrary barriers to Psyche's union with Amor, but also stages of purgation, necessary steps on the path that leads to that union. In the same way, the lower passional soul, the commanding *nafs*, though it must be overcome and in a sense 'killed', is in another sense divine and immortal, being an expression of God's general Mercy, *Rahman*, without which His particular, redeeming and reintegrating Mercy, *Rahim*, would have no field of operation. The *nafs* is the excess, the residue in the human psyche of God's act of universal creation—which, if it continues to expand and attenuate beyond the human state, the point where that creation is finished and complete, becomes the road to hell. The spiritual Path might be defined as the conscious turn, by the power of God's grace, from the path of creation, *Rahman*, to the path of *Rahim*, the return of all things to God. Thus the transformation of blind passion into human love is a reflection, in the world of the lesser or psychic mysteries, of the completion of the greater or spiritual mysteries: the reintegration of the human soul into its Divine Source.

In Amor, the particular personhood of the beloved is central—just as, in true spiritual realization, God is not an abstraction or an insubstantial wraith, but the most concrete Reality imaginable, one that is also infinitely beyond anything we can imagine. From the worldly point of view, love for particular persons is seen as mere bourgeois sentimentalism, whereas from a standpoint tinged with spiritual arrogance, love of the human beloved is viewed as mere idolatry, the worship of one's ego in the person of another. In the face of such worldly cynicism, and a (no less cynical) spiritual idealism, we are ashamed of romantic love. Just as the Victorians indulged in sentimental romance but hid their sexuality, so we indulge in every form of sexual exhibitionism, but are ashamed of Amor. In the words of the medieval German poet, Gottfried Von Strassburg, quoted by Joseph Campbell in his *Creative Mythology*:

> I pity Love with all my heart, for though almost all today hold and cleave to her, no one concedes to her her due. We all want our pleasure of her, and to consort with her. But no! Love is not what we, with our deceptions, are now making of her for each other. We are going at things the wrong way. We sow black henbane, and expect to reap lilies and roses. But, believe me, that cannot be.... It is really true what they say, 'Love is harried and hounded to the ends of the earth.' All that we possess of her is the word, her name alone remains to us; and that, too, we have so bandied about, misused and vulgarized, that the poor thing is ashamed of her name, disgusted with the very sound of it. She is cringing and flinching everywhere at her own existence. Misused and dishonored, she sneaks begging from

house to house, lugging shamefully a sack all of patches, crammed with her swag and booty, which she denies to her own mouth, and offers for sale in the streets. Alas! It is we who have created that market. We traffic with her in this amazing way and then claim to be innocent. Love, the queen of all hearts, the free-born, the one and only, is put up for public sale! What a shameful tribute is this that our mastery has required of her!

Here Gottfried shows how faithlessness in Amor leads to lust—the same complaint that was made about indiscriminate Agape in The Epistle of Jude, which denounces the excesses of the early Christian *agape* feasts.

In our present culture the image of human innocence, tenderness and self-sacrifice, especially in a woman, is literally terrifying to us, since it confronts us with the depth of our own self-betrayal. Sociologist Herbert Hendin, writing in 1975 when the present emotional regime was being established after the transitional period of the 60's, had this impression of the college students he studied:

> women...to shield themselves from male anger... attempt to create a life that seems expressly designed to rule out the possibility of being affected by a man. The fear of involvement is profound, pervasive...a fear of being totally wiped out, or losing the fight for self-validation... most young women avoid real intimacy with a man, feeling that caring itself is self-destructive...for both sexes in society, caring for anyone deeply is becoming synonymous with losing.... In a culture that institutionalizes lack of commitment, it is very hard to be committed; in a nation that seems determined to strip sex of romance and tenderness, it is very hard to be a tender and faithful lover. ('The Revolt Against Love', *Harper's Magazine*, August 1975)

Over thirty years later, this is still true, or even truer. And if Hendin's conclusions sound jarring to some ears, it is because the state of things he laments is now so taken for granted that his tone of outrage may seem a bit excessive. According to the

New Testament, this plague of emotional coldness is one of the signs of the 'latter days'. In the words of Jesus, 'because iniquity shall abound, the love of many shall wax cold' [Matt. 24:12].

In Amor are synthesized the passion of Eros and the generosity of Agape. But the vessel in which this synthesis takes place is not the realm of impersonal principles, but the particularity and holy limitation (transpersonal in essence) of interpersonal love. As the uniqueness of each individual reflects the incomparability of the Divine Essence, irrespective of the ontological level on which the reflection takes place, so each relationship of love between two human beings is, as it were, its own 'Name of God', to use the Islamic term; it is this understanding that led Emmanuel Swedenborg to say that a married couple appears, in the imaginal Eternity of the spiritual world, as a single angel. From the standpoint of *being* (Arabic *wujud*, that by which a thing *is*), the Names are ranged in ranks, some higher and some lower, according to their capacity to reflect something of the mystery of the Divine Nature. But in terms of *essence* (Arabic *mahiyya*, that by which a thing is *what* it is) each is unique (though without being isolated as a separate entity), which is why it is said that each Name of God contains all the others. When the perspective of *being* is veiled—when *what* something is takes precedence over *that* something is—the Names of God, and the human individuals and relationships that are these Names' reflections, become bound in their own limited forms, their 'egos'. They are 'merely' relative; they are opaque, eccentric—even vulgar—and so potentially idolatrous: idols to those who venerate them, idols also to their own self-worship. On the other hand, when the perspective of *essence* is veiled—when *that* something is takes precedence over *what* it is—the world of the Principles appears, but it remains abstract, and is therefore unable to redeem those relative forms fixed in their eccentricity and vulgarity. But when the perspective of Being and that of Essence are united, as in the alchemical *magnum opus*, then the Principles are embodied and concretely manifested in particular forms; and at the same time those forms are sublimated, annihilated in their 'egos', and so freed from their inherent limitations in conformity with their Principles.

Romantic love, in its fullest development, is a primary site of the marriage between Being and Essence, between Divine and human love. But this intrinsic and necessary relationship between the human and the Divine, which, mysteriously, is one both of strict hierarchical subordination and of a relationship between equals, as well as of complete and undifferentiated Union, is as difficult to understand in its full range of implications as are, for example, the allied doctrines of the two natures of Christ, or the ultimate identity of Transcendence and Immanence; we always seem to err in one direction or the other. Elias Jweied, in his article 'The Sophianic Vision' (*Studies in Tradition*, Autumn 1992)—under the section entitled 'The Derivative Beloved'—attempts to deal with this relationship between the human and the Divine when he confronts the question of who Dante's Beatrice really was:

> All too often, one finds in the commentaries on Dante a confusion as to who was the Beatrice of whom Dante's heart has so eloquently sung. On the one hand, the literary historians argue that it was Beatrice Portinari, the wife of a Florentine banker....on the other, there are people who say that Beatrice was simply a metaphor whose physical existence may never have been witnessed.

> However, both these positions miss the mark. There was a Beatrice whom Dante had physically seen. However, Dante's lyrics and Commedia are not for the love of this 'earthly' Beatrice. Rather, this Beatrice was, for Dante, that special individual who physically reveals a theophany to the *fedele* who in turn realizes that it was only the reflection of the One he really loves—in a word, this Beatrice was the mirror of the Beloved of Dante's mind....

This is certainly accurate to a particular valid mode of theophany. But we need to ask ourselves whether Dante himself ever would, or ever did, speak of Beatrice as 'only' a reflection of the One. Imagine Dante saying such a thing to her: 'My Lady, understand that it is not you I love, but the One reflected in you.' Or imagine him telling his friend Cavalcanti, 'this girl Beatrice is all very well as a derivative beloved; I'm sure I'll get an epic out of her at least. But of course she is only a means to an end.' If he had adopted this attitude, we can rest assured that the *Commedia* would never have been composed, even if some other jilted lover had not rewarded such crassness by dropping some aconite in his wine...

Equally revealing is Jweied's definition of the *fedele's* beloved as 'that special individual who *physically* reveals a theophany.' Certainly human physical beauty, as in Plato's *Symposium*, is an incomparable mirror of the Beauty of God—a truth which, under present social mores that either exploit a woman's (and, increasingly, a man's) physical beauty as crassly as possible, or attempt to suppress it as representing either a dangerous vulnerability or an unfair advantage, it takes courage as well as insight to admit. But cannot the *fedele's* beloved also act as a theophany of the Divine through her qualities of moral, intellectual and spiritual beauty? Are we asked to believe that if Beatrice had been a physically beautiful woman with a vicious soul—if, indeed, she were destined for damnation—Dante would still have been able to know her as the soul of his life and his life's work, the *Divine Comedy*? To believe this would be to accept the equivalent of the Apollinarian heresy in the realm of romance— which, in terms of christology, denied that Christ had an individual human soul, and therefore failed to recognize the spiritual import of the individual soul per se. Elsewhere in the article, Jweied compares Dante's relationship with Beatrice to Ibn al-'Arabi's with Nizam, the young daughter of a good friend at Mecca. But Nizam, for Ibn al-'Arabi, was more than simply a physical or visual mirror of the Divine Reality. He says of her:

Now this sheikh had a daughter, a lissome young girl who captivated the gaze of all who saw her, whose mere presence was the ornament of our gatherings and startled all who contemplated it to the point of stupefaction. The magic of her glance, the grace of her conversation were such an enchantment that when on occasion, she was prolix, her words flowed from the source: when she spoke concisely, she was a marvel of eloquence: when she expounded an argument, she was clear and transparent.... If not for the paltry souls who are ever ready for scandal and predisposed to malice, I should comment on the beauties of her body, which was a garden of generosity....

I took her as my model for the interpretation of the poems contained in the present book [*The Interpreter of Ardent Desires*], which are love poems, composed in suave, elegant phrases, although I was unable to express so much as a part of the emotion which my soul experienced and which the company of this young girl awakened in my heart, or of the generous love I felt, or of the impression which her unwavering friendship left in my memory, or of the grace of mind or the modesty of her bearing, since she is the object of my Quest and my hope, the Virgin Most Pure. Nevertheless, I succeeded in putting into verse some of the thoughts connected with my yearning, as precious gifts and objects which I here offer. I let my enamoured soul speak clearly, I tried to express the profound attachment I felt, the profound concern that tormented me in those days now past, the regret that still moves me at the memory of that noble society and that young girl.

Whatever name I may mention in this book, it is to her that I am alluding. Whatever the house whose elegy I sing, it is of her house I am thinking.

May God preserve the reader of this Diwan from any temptation to suppose things unworthy of souls who despise such vileness, unworthy of their lofty designs concerned solely with things celestial. Amen—by the power of Him who is the one Lord. (Henry Corbin, *Creative Imagination in the Sufism of Ibn 'Arabi*)

Clearly the mirror of theophany in this case is, paradoxically, at once the Reality Itself, and the human person—body, soul, personality and intellect—of the actual Nizam. Those who are familiar with Ibn al-'Arabi's doctrine of the interdependence of Lord and Servant, or God and Cosmos, as the polarized manifestation of the One Reality, will understand this. God does not manifest apart from His vessel, and this vessel is, in Essence though not in form, none other than that Reality. But if our understanding of this and analogous doctrines is not penetrating enough, then danger threatens, as Eias Jweied points out:

> One of the great dangers of the earthly theophany of God's beauty is the risk or forgetfulness and idolatry. More plainly speaking, if the vessel through which God pours his Beauty and Majesty is used for too long, before the *fedele* has become an experienced traveler upon the path of love, then he might grow too attached to the derivative beloved and may never spread the wings that were made to fly to the spheres. In such a circumstance he would become complacent, contented, and never achieve true happiness.

Idolatry of the human beloved is indeed a veil over the Reality, and an ever-present danger. But crassness toward her (or him) is equally a veil. If, in Jweied's words, the human beloved is *used* as a vessel of God's Beauty and Majesty instead of being *recognized* as such, the lover will be very unlikely to experience complacency or contentment, but will, on the contrary, attract to himself more of God's Rigor and Wrath than God's Beauty, as lovers in the habit of *using* their beloveds for this or that can well attest. In the realm of pure impersonal Eros, the spiritual equivalent of the 'one night stand' is entirely valid, since it is then a question not of the utilization of the beloved by the lover as a means to ascend to God, but more one of a free gift of the Grace of His Presence by God to the lover by means of the beloved. But in the world of Amor (and as soon as the arrow of Beatrice's glance entered Dante's heart, and lodged there, beyond hope of extraction in this life, it was a question of Amor, not Eros) the form of the beloved becomes, not only a momentary, but— mysteriously—also an eternal theophany of the Deity, since every moment of fully witnessed theophany, though in terms of time it passes, is nonetheless a moment of realized eternity. As glorified saints become forms of divine theophany beyond the stream of time (as both Eastern Orthodox *icons* and Vajrayana *thankas* attest), so also do unique moments of God's Self-revelation, and the forms through which such revelations occur (which, if we had eyes to see, would include every form and every moment). It was precisely the fact that Beatrice lent her form to a Divine theophany witnessed by Dante in this temporal world that allowed her to appear to him as an incarnation of Holy Wisdom in that other, eternal world.

We can perhaps understand this principle more easily if we compare the manifestation of God to Dante through Beatrice to His manifestation to the lands and peoples of Islam through the Prophet Muhammad, peace and blessings be upon him. No orthodox Muslim would describe a veneration of the person and *sunnah* of the Prophet as idolatry (though the literal deification of the Prophet and Ali by certain fringe groups would certainly qualify as such), and the same is true of a Sufi's veneration for his shaykh. Given that we are speaking of radically different levels of theophany, and in the understanding that the person and image of Beatrice were only a full theophany for Dante personally, I believe that the same principle applies to both (and God knows best). If one of the Prophet's companions had told him: 'I have no love for your earthly personality, I am merely using you as a ladder to Allah,' that companion would have missed one of the very ways in which the Prophet is able to function as just such a ladder. On the other hand, after the Prophet's death, Abu Bakr was fully justified in declaring to the assembly: 'If you worship Muhammad, know that he is dead. But if the One you worship is Allah, know that He will never die.' So the balance was struck.

But the balance between the human and the Divine beloved— or rather the recognition of true love itself as Divine in essence—cannot be achieved if the object of love is false. Human and Divine love can be synthesized because they are already one in essence. Sacred and profane love cannot, since love for a false object, even if ultimately derives from the Divine Source of all love, and is subjectively sincere, in objective terms is a case of idolatry which necessarily leads, eventually, to a hardening of the heart, and a heart encrusted with egotism cannot intuit Divine realities.

Frithjof Schuon, perhaps the greatest of the latter-day sages of the 'Traditionalist' school, correctly teaches that 'the theophanic quality of the human body resides uniquely in its form, not in the sanctity of the soul inhabiting it' (*From the Divine to the Human*, p92), and 'outward Beauty, even when combined with inner ugliness, testifies to Beauty as such' (*Stations of Wisdom*, p6). True! But this doctrine, though true, and therefore a valid element of a legitimate spiritual Way, desperately needs to be balanced by the doctrine that the very same beauty—as in the legend of White Buffalo Cow Woman—is either *vidya-maya* or *avidya-maya* depending upon our purity or impurity of heart, that if one is attracted to that vicious soul by means of that beautiful body, then one 'will not come out again until he has paid the last farthing.' Without a teaching which elucidates Eros in its false and rigorous as well as its true and merciful forms, a strict puritanism would be the wiser course. There are plenty of traditional sources (the Grimm's fairy tale 'The Goose Girl,' for example) which remind us that the outwardly attractive woman is not always the true bride, a doctrine which is valid in gnostic as well as emotional terms. Popular culture also recognizes this truth, its classic cinematic statement being the motion picture *The Blue Angel*, starring Marlene Dietrich. But it is Shakespeare, not surprisingly, who ultimately says it best.

In *The Merchant of Venice*, Portia—Divine Wisdom—has concealed her portrait in one of three caskets, one of gold, one of silver, and one of lead. She is then approached by three suitors. The expansive, foolish one chooses the gold casket: wrong. The cold, calculating one chooses the silver casket: wrong again. But the true bridegroom, Bassiano, chooses the leaden casket, and in so doing becomes a type of Christ, who endured the *tamasic* heaviness of the material world, death on the cross, and the harrowing of hell to save us. Within the lead of radical *kenosis*, he finds the portrait of the True Bride. 'You that choose not by the view' says Portia, 'chance as fair, and choose as true!' And we need to listen as well to her verse dismissing the Prince of Morocco, the vain, inflated suitor, whose character reminds one of the Islamic legend that it was the peacock—narcissistic aestheticism—who introduced the serpent into Paradise:

All that glisters is not gold,—
Often have you heard that told:
Many a man his life hath sold
But my outside to behold:
Gilded tombs to worms infold.
Had you been as wise as bold,
Young in limbs, in judgement old,
Your answer had not been inscroll'd:
Fare you well; your suit is cold.

Only the man, or woman, who thoroughly understands this can look upon Beauty naked, and know it as Wisdom. To teach 'Beauty is the splendor of the True' without at all points immediately balancing it with 'all that glisters is not gold' is to invoke *avidya-maya*, ultimately leading to the veiling of the Intellect and the corruption of the will. Beauty of body is indeed a theophany, and when Schuon exalts it, he is speaking truth, a truth which is a necessary and legitimate compensation for the ascetic hatred of beauty—as exhibited, for example, by the beautiful Christian saint who disfigured her face to discourage her many suitors—as well as for the general hatred of beauty, or even *fear* of it, which is an inescapable aspect of the collective human soul in these latter days. But someone whose intellect is pure and whose will is virtuous will necessarily experience a beautiful body coupled with a vicious soul as anomalous and inappropriate, this reaction being the trace within us of our primordial or Edenic state, when physical Beauty was the direct manifestation of Virtue, as Virtue was of Intelligence. A beautiful painting discovered in a garbage dump is a similar anomaly. Anyone of sound sensibilities will, upon encountering it, have two reactions: 'What a beautiful work of art!' and: 'What is such a beautiful work of art doing in a garbage dump?' Furthermore, if two exhibitions of beautiful paintings were announced in the papers, one taking place in a museum and the other in a garbage dump (something which is far from impossible nowadays, and may already have actually occurred, given the idolatry of ugliness of the contemporary art world), the person of sound sensibilities will choose the museum over the garbage dump, every time. The quest for beauty in human form, if it is a true quest, combining sincerity of intention and a goal which is one with objective Truth, must be the quest for the *fullness* of beauty: beauty of body, beauty of soul (virtue), and beauty of Spirit (intelligence). An exception to this imperative is the duty of the saint or spiritual guide who must attend to all aspects, Spirit, soul and body, of the person he is commanded by God to enlighten and sanctify—a process which entails, on the guide's part, a vicarious suffering, from a higher level of integration, of the comparative disintegration of the soul in his charge. (Even simple charity will, to a degree, require the same thing of any one of us.) And part of the charisma granted to the one whose duty it is to spiritually purge others within a context of guidance may be to contemplate, in a person whose soul is sick, physical beauty as a theophany of the Divine, thus putting that person at least virtually in touch with the spiritual integration he or she has heretofore failed to achieve, as in the case of the Sufi saint Ruzbehan Baqli, who fell in love with a singing-girl just long enough to awaken her to the Divine Beauty which had been veiled from her by her own profane relationship to beauty, after which God removed his infatuation.

Be that as it may, anyone whose ideal is something less than the fullness of Beauty has embarked on a centrifugal course. The fruit of the Tree of the Knowledge of Good and Evil has a degree of beauty, since it a reflection of Beauty Itself: this is the grain of truth in the serpent's lie that those who eat of it will become like God. But it is not the fullness of Beauty; it is not the Tree of Life. A man who rests content with beauty of body alone will necessarily experience it as *avidya-maya*. In contemplation of it, his virtue will become corrupted, his intelligence darkened. This is why it is spiritually incumbent upon us, when encountering a beautiful body coupled with a vicious soul, not to deny that this beauty is a revelation of Divine Beauty, but to turn away from that beauty in its incomplete and distorted form, just as one would not, in order to contemplate a beautiful painting, spend several hours in a garbage dump. One would either remove the painting from the dump, or, if this were not possible, turn and leave the premises.

Schuon often seems to identify the beauty of the human body with the beauty of nature. The manifestation of God through the human body, however, is on a different ontological level, and obeys different rules, than His manifestation in other natural forms. Men and women are not noble lions and beautiful gazelles—they are men and women: body, soul, and Spirit. The viciousness of the tiger is not at odds with its beauty, since they together manifest the mystery that God's Rigor is inherent in His Beauty, and His Beauty implicit in His Rigor. But in the case of the human being, beauty of form and viciousness of soul *are* at odds. If we are blind to this truth, if we forget the warning, from the *I Ching*, that 'sincerity toward disintegrating influences is dangerous', if we turn aside from the quest for the fullness of beauty to contemplate beauty of body coupled with viciousness of soul, then our awareness will necessarily be diverted away from the viciousness, which is repulsive, and toward the beauty, which is attractive, the result being that we will begin to see the person in question not as a human being, but as a *body*, albeit a body which is also, and legitimately so, a theophany. At this point, we have become partners-by-default of the Manichaeans, in that we have introduced a radical dualism between body and soul, and have also forgotten in the process that a viciousness of soul will always leave traces—sometimes subtle, sometimes grossly obvious—in the gait, in the physiognomy, in the tone of voice. Furthermore, the attempt to contemplate Beauty as separate from sound traits of soul such as justice, compassion, humility and courage is to transform it from a manifestation of Divine Gentleness, Innocence and Mercy into one of Divine Wrath: there is nothing more wrathful than a cold beauty, like that of the cobra hypnotizing its victim, which doubtless attracts, but attracts only to destruction. And it is not essentially lust which is attracted to such cold beauty: it is pride. The belief that one can separate beauty of form from viciousness of soul, and contemplate it alone while coming to no harm, is inseparable from the sort of pride which believes that, *through power* rather than through intelligence and virtue, it can extract the juice of life and discard the rind. Schuon is aware of the dangers of unchastity in the contemplation of the beauty of the human form; he is less aware—at least one gets this impression—of the dangers of aesthetic pride.

And what becomes of the human soul which is ignored and neglected in the name of a contemplation of the human body? If we do not see others in their full humanity, then we 'murder' them, and destroy as well the fullness of our own humanity. As beautiful bodies whose souls remain invisible to us, they may be supports for our *own* contemplation of God, but it becomes progressively less possible for us to imagine them as contemplators in their own right. We forget that the 'I' within us, though obviously unique, is mysteriously one with the equally unique 'I's' within them; consequently, what Schuon calls 'the mystery of multiple subjectivities' becomes veiled, and the beautiful objects in question become transformed from theophanies of the Divine into possessions of the ego.

It is, in fact, an incipient pride, egotism and hard-heartedness that attracts one to a false object of love in the first place. Jennifer Doane Upton, in *Dark Way to Paradise: Dante's Inferno in Light of the Spiritual Path*, speaks of the dichotomy between true and false love:

> While Dante wrote profoundly about spiritual love, he certainly knew intimately the dangers of false love. He composed a series of poems dedicated to a woman named *Pietra*, 'stone', who totally captivates his heart even though she is cruel and in no way returns his affections. Because all the warmth in him goes out to her, but finds nothing kindred in her to respond to it, he is, through this experience, *petrified*, just as he comes close to being turned to stone by the Medusa in Canto IX of the *Inferno*.

He is of course describing in these poems the experience of being psychologically destroyed through fascination, which is equally dangerous whether it be for a false woman or a false philosophy. What is it, then, which makes his affection for this woman so different than his love for Beatrice, who also fascinated him, and who, at least on an earthly level, did not reciprocate his feelings?

In the *Purgatorio*, Beatrice rebukes Dante for having permitted his attention to stray to other women (or false philosophies) instead of allowing it, when she died, to follow her to her grave. Superficially his attraction to the stone woman and his love for Beatrice are similar, but inwardly the difference is immense, since, through Beatrice, Dante comes face to face with Divine Mercy itself, whose archetypal symbol within the poem is the Virgin Mary. He gives his attention to that Mercy, which has given visions of the Virgin to so many—and since he has first given, he is now able to receive such grace from that Mercy, which is finally the Virgin herself, that the very darkest places in his soul are illuminated. After all, did not Beatrice, who is a substitute for the Virgin, leave her footprint in Hell? Through his vision of Beatrice, those wounds to his soul which were caused by his propensity to yield to profane fascination are healed.

At what place, and in what time, did Dante's fascination for the stone-hearted woman end, and his love for Beatrice, which is a path to Divine Love, begin? Even though Dante describes the beginning of this love in *La Vita Nuova*, the reader does not really know the true time and place of this love's awakening, because that is a secret of the soul. The true time and place of the birth of his love for Beatrice are at the point where the Divine Mercy itself came into his life and penetrated into its innermost depths. The senses do not know about this event; it is the soul alone which hears it.

Ralph Austin, in his article 'The Feminine Dimension of Ibn al-'Arabi's Thought' (*Journal of the Muhyiddin Ibn 'Arabi Society*, volume 2, 1984), also strikes the true balance—temporarily at least—between the earthly and the Divine beloved. He says, of Ibn al-'Arabi's *The Interpreter of Ardent Desires*,

> Here all the threads of his vision of the feminine dimension of Reality come together in a wonderfully synthetic image in which a powerful sensuousness mingles with a rare wisdom, and in which all the combined attraction of fascination of the earthly and essential feminine fuses to illustrate brilliantly what H. Corbin has called the Sympathy of matter and spirit in the mutual inter-dependence of substance and concept, actuality and virtuality which is such an important characteristic of Ibn al-'Arabi's view and which so often bewilders the reader.

Further on, however, he loses his balance again, directly contradicting his earlier statement:

> Ibn al-'Arabi is not concerned with the personal and individual Nizam, but with the trans-personal archetype, albeit reflected, in the instance of his meeting with Nizam, in a particular human woman; that is to say, he is interested and affected by her only in so far as her person is a medium of supra-human realities . . . the women as subject or as symbolic of the divine Subject does not enter into his scheme of things.

One need only refer to Ibn al-'Arabi's own description of his feelings for Nizam, quoted above (and which Prof. Austin quotes in his own article) to see the error in this view. To state it succinctly, one cannot simply take the archetype and dump the woman, since it is only the lover's interest in the 'personal and individual female' that allows the 'trans-personal archetype' to manifest, just as it is only the manifestation of the archetype that exempts the love of the individual woman from the charge of idolatry. As Jennifer Doane Upton has written, speaking of romantic literature:

We can miss the spirituality of a romantic story in two ways. One is to take it simply as a human love story, and not allow any realization of the spiritual dimension of human love to arise. The other is to treat it merely as an allegory, and try to cut out the human, the romantic level. Often those with some spiritual insight will relate to romantic material in just this way. If they see that the story is pointing toward higher realities, they believe they can ignore the human level and concentrate on the level of spiritual allegory alone. However, if one is not a romantic, one cannot reach a spiritual level of understanding by means of romantic literature.

Just before the last passage quoted, Prof. Austin had been speaking of the contemporary resurgence of archetypal femininity through feminism on the one hand and pornography on the other, and had expressed the opinion (undoubtedly correct!) that Ibn al-'Arabi would probably not have approved of these developments, so he is probably just being a bit over-zealous here. But when Ibn al-'Arabi says, 'May God preserve the reader of this Diwan from any temptation to suppose things unworthy of souls who despise such vileness, unworthy of their lofty designs concerned solely with celestial realities', he is not saying that he cares nothing for Nizam as a person, but is simply defending himself against the charge that his Diwan was composed in order to seduce, or publish the sexual conquest of, the lovely young daughter of his host. Here we can see how the prevalence of pornography in our culture has apparently driven Prof. Austin into the realms of abstract metaphysics in an attempt to take refuge from the all-pervasive cultural vileness, and how such impersonal elevation is in fact no refuge at all, since it is still next to impossible for him to see the *personal* Nizam as anything other than a potential object of lust.

Elias Jweied, in the article discussed above, quotes Prof. Austin as maintaining that

the human gender of the beloved does not really matter, for, in the words of Rumi ... it is higher than male or female.

Secondly, however, the Feminine has been associated with the whole phenomenon of love, passion and beauty so that . . . it is the feminine symbol which dominates.

Once again, the feeling-nuance of this passage leaves something to be desired. To begin with, while it is true that either sex can legitimately function as a mirror of the Divine Beloved, since the Godhead completely transcends sexuality, but this does not make the genders simply interchangeable. For Dante, the human gender of the beloved mattered 'quasi-absolutely'; no man could have taken the place of Beatrice. Likewise, for Rumi, no woman could have replaced Shams al-Din Tabrizi. For Majnun there was only Layla, a woman; for Zuleikha, only Yusuf, a man. The denial of this theophanic necessity is entirely in line with the contemporary 'liberal' tendency to suppress all gender differences, in order to undermine the family as an integral unity of society, to further the mechanization of reproduction, and to subvert the man-woman polarity so that it can no longer function as a central symbol of celestial and Divine realities in the collective mind. As Prof. James Cutsinger, basing his position largely on the teachings of Frithjof Schuon, writes in his article 'Femininity, Hierarchy and God' (from *Religion of the Heart: Essays Presented to Frithjof Schuon on his Eightieth Birthday*), the polarity of gender 'is to be found . . . all the way up to and in the Divine Reality itself . . . which is the ultimate Source of everything else, and which for that reason is the source and paradigm of all distinctions. In its absoluteness and transcendence, the Divine is the archetype of everything masculine, while its infinity and capacity for immanence are displayed at every level of the feminine'. Furthermore, while the feminine is in one sense the principle of relatedness (intrinsically, not just by social convention) by virtue of its kinship with the Divine Immanence, such relatedness can never come into play while its fundamental polar relationship with the masculine principle is denied. Without the discriminating function of the masculine principle, the feminine principle is not relatedness, only mutual identification.

III

The destruction of love does not always begin with a perversion of human intent; it may also happen because the social and psychological context that would allow a genuine loving intent to express itself has disappeared. We do not necessarily become selfish and unloving out of a desire to gain advantage; we may simply find ourselves being punished by the prevailing psychosocial forces for acting in a loving manner. Our selfishness and coldness start as 'legitimate' acts of self-preservation. But without love we cannot live as human beings. And this is one of the central ironies of the latter days: that in order to survive, we must (apparently) sacrifice more and more of the things that are necessary to our survival—just as, in order to subsist on earth, we must (under the present system of things) progressively destroy the earth.

The disappearance of love, then, has everything to do with the destruction of the Matrix of love; and in order to expand on this theme, I will need to take some time to better define 'Matrix' as a metaphysical principle.

One of the hardest-to-define spiritual qualities, or Divine hypostases—at least in these latter days—is the one I am calling Matrix. Since it is the most perfectly granted of all spiritual qualities, it is precisely the one that we are most likely to take for granted. It is definitely a manifestation of the feminine pole of Divinity, but it is not *shakti*, neither the all-manifesting *shakti* of God, which Muslims call *nafas ar-Rahman*, 'the Breath of the Merciful', (*Rahman* being God's all-creating and all-permitting general mercy), nor the all-reintegrating redemptive *shakti* of God— in Muslim terms, *Rahim*, God's particular mercy, the mercy of orientation-toward-center, the principle of the spiritual Path. It is neither exactly the Hindu *avidya-maya*, the principle of cosmic manifestation insofar as it veils its own Source, nor *vidya-maya*, the principle of revelation, of manifestation insofar as it leads all things back to that Source. All these hypostases of the Divine Feminine are dynamic in one way or another, while Matrix is profoundly at rest, and empty. And this very emptiness is the site-of-manifestation of Divine Love, which relates the concept of Matrix to that of the Buddhist *prajña*, that pristine, empty, all-informing Wisdom which is inseparable from Compassion, as its mythic representations as the goddesses Prajñaparamita or Tara or Kwan-Yin demonstrate (though, in Vajrayana Buddhism, Compassion per se is related to the active masculine rather than the passive feminine pole, which is identified with Wisdom.)

Frithjof Schuon speaks of the Divine Essence as intelligible in terms of the polarity of the Absolute, from which the masculine principle springs, and the Infinite, which gives rise to the feminine principle. By virtue of its Infinity, the Absolute radiates, unfolding universal manifestation; by virtue of Its Absoluteness, Infinite manifestation never fundamentally departs from its own nature, never becomes *essentially* other than God. The Absolute is related to the transcendence of God, the Infinite to God's immanence. But although Matrix is in one sense precisely the Infinite, in another it is a direct reflection of the Essence Itself in manifest conditions, without direct reference to the polarity Absoluteness/Infinity as Schuon most often presents it. It is both Absolute and Infinite, being Absolute without aloofness and Infinite without radiation and extension. It is the 'field' aspect of God, the Divine considered as totally undifferentiated Substance. It is God's Immanence, by which That One is present in all things, not because He is identified with them, or because He is hidden inside them, but because He absolutely transcends them. If universal manifestation is necessarily feminine in relation to God's creative act conceived of as masculine, then we can say that all the particular 'contents' of Matrix are necessarily masculine in relation to the 'space' in which they eternally exist, conceived of as feminine. Mythopoetically speaking, as the night sky is the Queen of Heaven, so the stars, the 'host of heaven', are Her sons. In Vajrayana terms, the empty space of Wisdom is *prajña*, in relation to which the Means of attaining wisdom, *upaya*, are seen as active, masculine, and manifest in terms of time rather than space—though no less eternal for all that.

Matrix is gestalt, where 'figure' is the Absolute symbolized as a single point, and 'ground' the field of the Infinite. It is 'an

infinite sphere whose center is everywhere and whose circum-
ference is nowhere.' Formless in itself, it is informing context.
Seen in terms of Matrix, God is not so much the Creator of all
things as the Absolute Context of all things.

Matrix (in Cha'an Buddhist terms) is 'the Void eternally gen-
erative.' It is the all-embracing, perfectly empty Divine Space
that allows all things to be exactly as they are. It is *shunyata* (void-
ness), hostess to *tathata* (suchness). In the highest sense it is the
Essence Itself, Beyond Being. In the intermediate sense, it is
Beyond Being pregnant with all the 'minute particulars' of possible Being. Again, if these particulars are symbolized by the stars,
Matrix is best represented by the blackness of the night sky. In
the lowest sense, it is cosmic manifestation considered *sub specie
aeternitatis*, in terms of the 'simultaneity' of all-encompassing
Space rather than the eternally creative and re-integrative Time
which flows through it. It is not time; it is that which allows
time to pass. It is related to *Rahman* in that it allows all things to
exist, but it is not an outbreathing. It is like *Rahim* in that it
allows for orientation, discriminative justice, and the choice of
the Way, but it itself is impartial and undivided. It is the principle behind *Maya*, both manifesting *avidya-maya* and reintegrative
vidya-maya, but in itself it is not *Maya*. (Nonetheless, though
Matrix is the principle from which *Maya* itself emanates, in both
its *vidya* and *avidya* forms, it bears a special relationship to the latter, since *vidya-maya* reveals it, while *avidya-maya* obscures it.) If
Maya is a fishnet, Matrix is the space seen through the mesh. It is
empty. It is that which is not affected by the outbreathing and
inbreathing of the Absolute, the day and night of Brahma. It is
aether in its highest sense of totally unmanifest Substance. It is
'the face of the waters' in Genesis, considered as completely
unchanged by God's creative Spirit moving upon it. It is not the
waves; it is the water itself. In Christian terms it is the Virgin
Mary, whose highest aspect, symbolic of the Essence, is the
Black Virgin. In Islamic terms it is Fatima ('the mother of her
father'). In specifically Sufi terms, it is Layla.

When Matrix manifests on the psychic, the subtle material,
the ecological and the social planes, it is the principle of all relat-

edness. On the psychic plane—speaking in alchemical terms—if the Absolute is reflected as Sulfur and the Infinite as Mercury, Matrix is the principle of Salt, or of the *athenor*, the alchemical vessel. On the subtle material level it is the energy or field-aspect of biological life. On the ecological level, it is the balance of nature. On the social level, it is the system of harmonious interpersonal relations.

In terms of the Hindu *trimurti* it is Vishnu, insofar as he encompasses and transcends both creation and destruction. The *I Ching* defines the Tao as 'that which allows now light, now darkness to appear'—and so it is the Tao, the 'valley spirit' that 'never dies' in the *Tao Te Ching*. In it, all manifest things are as if they were never manifested; all forms are void. Before being emanated from their Principle, and before returning to it, in Matrix all things are one with their Principle now: 'all beings are enlightened from the beginning.'

Matrix is that which allows all things to relate to one another without acting to unite them. It in there are no barriers to relatedness. From the standpoint of Matrix it can be seen that those things which are attracted to each other and those which are repelled from each other are equally related. It is infinite detachment. It is infinite love.

Matrix in the absolute sense is the Principle of an indefinite number of relative matrices of which manifest existence, speaking in subtle terms, is composed. Each relative matrix is the set of all the relationships, actions and events that are possible within it. Thus the matrix or a given group or organization, for example, will allow space for certain thoughts and feelings and deny this space to others. (The reason I speak of thoughts and feelings here rather than actions is that the parameters of acceptable action are determined by explicit rules, while the acceptability of thoughts and feelings is determined implicitly by the surrounding relative matrix, just as a particular climate will allow for the development of certain plant and animal species but not others.)

According to René Guénon, as the present cycle of manifestation descends toward ultimate dissolution, the experience of existence in terms of space progressively gives way to its experience in terms of time—ever-accelerating time. Due to this development, it becomes increasingly difficult for us to sense the quality of Matrix. What was once so obvious a reality that it required no verbal definition progressively became so hidden from us that any intimation of it grew more and more difficult to entertain; and as a clear philosophical description of it consequently became more necessary, it also became harder to produce.

Matrix is what makes all relationship possible. When Matrix is unveiled, relationship takes place with no effort, just as it takes no effort for two rocks in a Zen garden to rest in perfect juxtaposition. But when Matrix is veiled, no amount of suffering or sacrifice or communication or passionate embrace can bring two people, two groups, two emotional qualities, or two ideas together. No man, by his own effort, can join together what God, by his perceived absence, has put asunder.

Ralph Austin, in the article already alluded to, renders the truth of what I am calling Matrix in a passage of rare depth. Commenting on Ibn al-'Arabi's own commentary on the hadith of Muhammad, 'Three things in this world have been made beloved to me: women, perfume and prayer', where the Shaykh al-Akbar sees in this statement man's intermediate position between the Divine Essence (*Dhat*, feminine gender) from which he springs and the human woman who springs from him—undoubtedly a reference to Eve, who was born from Adam's rib, and similar also to William Blake's understanding of the female consorts of his visionary gods as their 'emanations'—Austin says:

> this microcosmic triad is indeed a reflection of a greater, namely one in which Allah, the creating God, the first and supreme Name, is between His own secret Essence which, from the eternal treasury of latency, provides Him with the content of His Knowledge of Himself as creation and the created Cosmos, and the world which comes from him; or between his own latent wisdom, Sophia, and the universal

Nature which is the theatre of His infinite self-manifestation and elaboration. Thus, both macrocosmically and *in divinis*, man in the first instance and the worshipped God in the second, look upon two objects regarded as symbolically feminine, one the inner and essential, a hidden and secret mystery, the treasure of being, the other outward, apparently other and multiple, both of them providing a mirror to the observing subject, as also to each other, the one showing the reflection of potential illusion in the mirror of essential reality, the other the reflection of reality in the mirror of illusion, the one summoning to the isolation of uniqueness and peerlessness, the other to cosmic plurality and relativity. Also, at the divine level, both objects symbolize Infinitude, the one infinite virtuality or potentiality, latent and essential, the other of infinite actuality and becoming.

I hesitate to tamper with a passage of such nut-like concentration and sweetness; it remains only to say that, in line with Eckhart's dictum that 'the eye through which I see God and the eye through which He sees me is the same eye,' the two mirrors, that of cosmos and that of essence, are ultimately one—'sangsara is Nirvana' as the Mahayana Buddhists say—and this single infinite Mirror is what I mean by Matrix.

James Cutsinger, in 'Femininity, Hierarchy and God', speaks of femininity as 'a magnetic and deliquescent force'; and this is indeed one of the modes of the feminine, both cosmically and *in divinis*. But femininity as Matrix does not dissolve forms, nor attract our consciousness beyond forms to the Formless, but rather allows all forms to perfectly be, thus dissolving our egoic attachments to them, and by so doing transforming them into empty, crystalline and mirror-like apparitions of That which transcends them.

We might define Matrix as 'static, as opposed to dynamic, Infinity', as 'Infinity in repose'. Frithjof Schuon speaks of this aspect of the Divine Feminine in his chapter 'The Wisdom of Sayyidatna Maryam' from *Dimensions of Islam*:

the Virgin personifies Equilibrium, since she is identifiable
with the Substance of Harmony and Beauty . . . she personifies the receptive or passive perfection of universal Substance; but she likewise incarnates—by virtue of the
formless and occult nature of the Divine *Prakriti*—the inef-
fable essence of wisdom or spirituality, the both maternal
and virginal *prima materia* of all formal coagulations of the
Spirit. . . . Specifically, Marian spirituality may be summa-
rized in these terms: to become pure prayer, or pure receptivity before God.

In the same chapter Schuon identifies the Virgin with both
'the supreme *Shakti*' and 'the heavenly *Prajñaparamita*', and both
of these identifications are thoroughly justified. But I have felt it
important to differentiate between these two aspects, to bring
out as precisely as possible what I mean by the term Matrix. In
Hindu Tantra, the adamantine, formless and motionless Absolute is masculine—*Shakta*—and the infinite, dynamic power of
the Absolute—*Shakti*—is feminine, while for the Buddhist
Tantra the reverse is true: motionless Wisdom is feminine—
prajña—and the active Means for the realization of Wisdom is
masculine—*upaya*. In the New Testament, *Shakti* appears as
Herod's daughter Salome, the dancer, who veils herself to manifest the universe and unveils to dissolve it—and this is mythopoetically accurate despite the fact that, in the Gospels, she
represents the lowest and most destructive form of *avidya-
maya*—while *prajña* is the Virgin Mary, whose essence is serenity
(though, as Schuon points out, a serenity not unrelated to Rigor,
as impartiality is not unrelated to Justice, basing this on three
lines from the Magnificat, Luke 1:50–52). The Virgin, as Matrix,
does not dance—and yet Matrix, in its hidden essence, is not
other than *Shakti*, since it is precisely God's passive receptivity to
His own creative impulse that allows Him to manifest the cosmos; this is what it is meant in Genesis 2:1 when it is said that 'the
Spirit of God moved upon the face of the waters.'
Nonetheless, the distinction between *Shakti* and Matrix has
important consequences, since if, in line with Schuon's most

commonly-used model, the Hindu Tantric one, we view the Divine Feminine only as dynamic Infinity, overflowing with a superabundance of contingent forms—in other words, as *Shakti*—then to hold to any one of these ultimately illusory forms is idolatry, blind egotism, ignorance, and carries its own automatic karmic retribution—just as, if one holds to a rock in the center of a stream, one will automatically be battered by the current. From this viewpoint, love of the small, the particular, the circumscribed—as, for example, the love of a particular human person—is a doomed illusion, best deliberately sacrificed before it is painfully wrenched from one's grasp. But from the point-of-view of static, spatial Infinity, or Matrix—Schuon's Marian Equilibrium—the opposite conclusion may be reached: that, since Matrix, the all-encompassing, can in no way be encompassed, our only way of participating in this Infinite Reality is through the minute particulars of our lives, which, because they are absolutely incapable of aspiring to or rivaling Infinity, are capable of being, as it were, the crystallizations of that Infinity in the here and now. As the Divine Logos, 'without whom was not made anything that was made,' is mysteriously present in the Eucharist under the species of bread and wine, so that all-creative Word of the Father, whose tiniest sparks are the whirling galaxies, is present in our 'mere humanity', in the little things of which our lives are made, and without which we could not live. This is the reality that Matrix unveils: 'Whatever ye do unto the least of these, my brethren, ye do unto Me.' And the essence of these little things is also the truth of human relatedness. So, once again, the Divine Feminine as Matrix, or static Infinity, is the principle of all relatedness, the Space that gives *Shakti*, or cosmic attraction, her room to dance.

From this viewpoint we can see human love, and especially married love, not as a mere fascination which can be used to access the Divine level and then be discarded, as quickly as possible, but both as a means of reaching God and a way by which God reaches us—in other words, a sacrament.

So if Matrix, in terms of its earthly, psycho-social manifestation, is now being destroyed, how can we reverse this process?

James Cutsinger, in 'Femininity, Hierarchy and God', writes as follows:

> ours ... is an era of density and hardness, of heaviness and eclipse: It is the *Kali Yuga* or 'Dark Age'. The doors of perception have *not* been cleansed, men and women have come not merely to doubt or disbelieve but to deny the reality of higher worlds. Or if they still do believe, their faith is without the traditional complement of knowledge and reason, and it is directed toward a realm of shadows, seemingly no more real, and often less, than the plane of matter, whose phenomenal contingency and fragility they seldom glimpse, and then forget. 'In this state,' warns Schuon, the 'soul is at the same time as hard as stone and as pulverized as sand, it lives in the dead rinds of things and not in the Essence, which is Life and Love; it is at once hardness and dissolution.'
>
> What such a soul needs in part, what modern man needs is a means of melting—what Schuon calls 'the spiritual liquefaction of the *ego*'. And for this it needs the feminine. Theophanic, maieutic, recollective, and freeing, the role of the feminine must be to transport a mind grown too attached and masculine from exterior through interior to superior, by exposing that mind—again in the words of Schuon—to 'the warm, soft quality of spring, or that of fire melting ice and restoring life to frozen limbs.'

This is a true diagnosis and a wise prescription. I in no way intend to contradict it, but rather expand upon it, since the essentially alchemical metaphor Schuon and Cutsinger apply to the collective psyche is the royal road from metaphysical knowledge to its psychophysical application.

If we are to diagnose and prescribe for the psyche, either individual or collective, in alchemical terms, we must remember that the 'humors' are not two, but four, and that the archetypes that produce them, Sulfur and Mercury, each manifest in two modes, making four in all. On a certain level, the alchemical Sulfur represents the Spirit, and the alchemical Mercury the psyche or soul. But on the psychic plane itself, which is where alchemical metaphors are most completely applicable, Sulfur and Mercury, at least in their initial state, represent fallen powers of the soul in need of redemption, each one possessing within it the principle of that redemption, but both requiring this principle to be awakened and actualized via the alchemical Work, as initiated and sustained by God's grace. As fallen psychic powers, Sulfur is 'intellect in bondage to the will', while Mercury is 'will in bondage to the affections'. The 'sulfurous' personality is intellectually self-willed; the 'mercurial' one is capricious, incapable of any stable intent. And so unredeemed Sulfur corresponds in many ways to the personality of an immature man, Mercury to that of a childish woman.

According to Titus Burckhardt, the two modes of archetypal Sulfur are fixation and volatilization, and of Mercury, coagulation and dissolution. When the soul is in a state of equilibrium, which renders it 'virginally' receptive to the Spirit, volatilizing Sulfur is married to coagulating Mercury, and fixing Sulfur to dissolving Mercury. In an imbalanced or fallen state, on the other hand, fixing Sulfur unites with coagulating Mercury, producing the 'hardness' spoken of by Schuon, while volatilizing Sulfur unites with dissolving Mercury, producing 'pulverization and dissolution'. In psychological terms, the first condition corresponds to fanaticism or Puritanism, the second to relativism and libertinism, both moral and philosophical. Furthermore, as Burckhardt points out, these two states very often coexist in the same soul (and, I would add, the same society), producing the dangerous instability of the fanatic, and the jadedness and dryness of the debauchee.

So while it is true to say that the hardness of the contemporary ego needs to be liquefied, it is equally true that the chaos of the affections needs to be stabilized. In terms of the alchemical regime, if Sulfur is to fix capricious Mercury so that the soul can more fully reflect the principial domain, Mercury must first 'solve' the incomplete and imbalanced fixations of Sulfur, its willful attachments and fixed ideas. And if Mercury is to temper and 'incarnate' the mental volatility of Sulfur, Sulfur must first give Mercury a fixed an incandescent point toward which to flow. In other words, if the rational mind is to tame the affections, the affections must first moisten and vivify the mind. And if the affections are to help thought become fully three-dimensional and effective in actual life, thought must first show them a truth outside themselves to which they can become devoted, otherwise they will freeze into a state of sullen self-involvement. Furthermore, every stage of the inner alchemical regime is also a step in the development and purification of interpersonal relations. Alchemy is the courtesy of the psyche's relationship to the Spirit; courtesy is the alchemy of the relationship between one human being and another. And the essential scripture, in the West, of this twofold course is Wolfram's *Parzival*.

In one sense, Mercury, the feminine pole, can be seen as the psychic reflection of the Divine Love, and Sulfur, the masculine, of the Divine Intellect. But if we push this correspondence too far (as some of the Jungians have done), then what becomes of love *between* the sexes? If love is woman's work, and thought the province of men, then where can the sexes meet? At this point we need to remember that the magnetic pole of all psychic and spiritual development is the Divine Essence, in which intellect and love are one. In light of this we can see that love is not served only by the dissolution of hardened egotism but also by the intimation of transcendent Truth, by the disciplining of the emotions, and by the grounding and embodiment of the thoughts (although, from a wider perspective, all four of these developments can be seen as aspects of the conquest of egotism). A person imprisoned in a willful and petrified mindset cannot love—but neither can someone who has no sense of any truth outside himself, nor one whose emotions are chaotic, nor one who is possessed by abstract thoughts he is unable to realize. So the full service of Love entails the completion of the entire alchemical regime, the *magnum opus*. And what truly serves love equally serves knowledge, while what wounds love also darkens the intellect. If we have never learned to love others by knowing them, and know them through loving them, then we will not succeed in the Divine realm after having failed in the human one [cf. I John 4:20], since we ultimately know others with God's Knowing, and love them with His Love.

And the spiritual quality—or if it is permissible to express it in these terms, the Divine Hypostasis—that allows the alchemical *opus* to be completed is, precisely, *Matrix*. Matrix is the *athenor*, the *vas*, the only vessel, or sanctuary, in which the double marriage of volatilizing Sulfur with coagulating Mercury and fixing Sulfur with dissolving Mercury, (reminiscent of the double marriage at the end of the *Parzival* romance) can take place. And if the motionlessly active agent of the Great Work is Sulfur, and the actively receptive agent, Mercury, the vessel or *informing context* in which their marriage is concluded is *Salt*. Mary (Miriam, Maryam), is the Salt of the Work—which is why her name is etymologically related to the Latin *mare*, 'sea'. She is at once the vibratory Waves of *Shakti*, and the Salt whereby Sulfur and Mercury, like the Divine and human natures of Christ, are drawn together into hypostatic union.

IV

If we are going to elaborate a *metaphysic* and a *gnosis* of Divine and human love, however, we will have to confront at one point the tendency among many metaphysicians, including those of the Traditionalist/Perennialist School, to look at love as 'mere' affection, and *gnosis* as the polar opposite of love, as well as its ontological and epistemological superior. This tendency certainly appears in the works of Frithjof Schuon and René Guénon, who often place love in the shadow of spiritual knowledge in terms of the Path, as if love were limited to a sentimental and passionate *bhakti*, clearly inferior to a sober, elevated and all-comprehensive *jñana*—though both also speak of love as intrinsic to spiritual knowledge, as we have already seen, and will see more of below. Nonetheless, a subtle and pervasive bias apparently exists, among many with a sophisticated understanding of metaphysical principles, against a full integration of love, especially *human* love, into the spiritual Path—a bias which may have resulted in a real need to transcend sentimental religiosity, not to mention sexual lust, but which is nonetheless entirely in line with the postmodern world's hatred of romanticism, sentiment and human tenderness in any form.

René Guénon, in his study of the degeneration of the western notion of the 'heart' that appears in *Symbols of the Sacred Science*, says quite rightly that the earlier idea of the heart as the seat of the seamless union of Love with the Transcendent Intellect progressively degenerated, under the influence of rationalism, to the point where the heart was considered to be the principle of affectivity alone, devoid of intelligence, the seat of 'heat' without 'light'. Intelligence, now reduced to mere rationality, 'cold like the lunar light which is its symbol' in Guénon's words, was understood as pertaining only to the brain. 'In the order of principles, on the contrary' he says, 'these two aspects [i.e. intelligence and love, or light and heat], like all complementaries, meet and are united, for they are constituents of one and the same essential nature.'

Guénon, however, sometimes takes the opposite tack, tending to see the spiritual intellect as central and love as peripheral; apparently he only intermittently understood the Spirit of God as a seamless unity of Love and Knowledge, as Dante clearly did in the last cantos of the *Paradiso*. In the earlier iconography of the radiant heart, before rationalism removed the seat of intelligence from the heart to the brain, Guénon discerned 'an acknowledged preponderance of the luminous aspect' (intelligence), and also maintained that

> when fire is polarized into ... light [Guénon's symbol of intelligence] and heat [his symbol of love], they are, so to speak, in an inverse ratio to one another ... and it is common knowledge ... that the less light a flame gives the hotter it is.

But, of course, this is generally not the case. Hotter stars are more brilliant than colder ones, and one of the hottest chemical fires we know, that of rapidly oxidizing magnesium, is also one of the brightest, burning with an incandescent, pure white flame. And given that Guénon also identifies heat with *life* as well as love, how far is his position, really, from that of D.H. Lawrence—the perfect example of an over-cerebral modern western man seeking the lost side of his humanity in the darkness of instinctive passion—when he said: 'KNOWING and BEING are opposite, antagonistic states. The more you know, exactly, the less you *are*. The more you *are*, in being, the less you know'? Both Guénon and Lawrence are right when speaking of intelligence when reduced to rationality and love when reduced to sentiment; an excessive attachment to rational thought does indeed repress emotion and sensation, just as an excessive attachment to sentiment makes us foolish and irrational. But *if* Guénon is saying that intelligence and love vary inversely *in the realm of principles*, then he is wrong. In the spiritual Heart, any increase in love is an increase in intelligence, and any increase in intelligence is an increase in love. Love of God is inseparable from knowledge of God, since to know Him is to love Him, and love of God is inseparable from knowledge of Him, since love is intimacy, and intimacy is the perfection of knowledge; *gnosis* itself may accurately be defined as 'concrete, *intimate* knowledge'.

Guénon also maintained that 'the ancients represented love as blind.' Apodictic statements like this, so common in Guénon's writings, lead us to lament his notorious lack of sufficient *documentation*: exactly who are these 'ancients', exactly how, either iconographically or textually, did they represent love as blind, and exactly what sort of 'love' were they talking about? Certainly the Greek tragedies are enough to prove that much was known in antiquity about the damage that blind passion and *hubris* can do; and yet to simply say 'the ancients represented love as blind' is incorrect. Plato's *Symposium*, to take only one example, is based on the doctrine that Eros, defined as an attraction to Beauty, is in fact the path to the highest intellectual illumination. And to the degree that the Hindu *Maya*—certainly an ancient doctrine—may be taken to be the product of 'love' in the sense of attachment to form, we need to clearly distinguish between *avidya-maya*, the product of blind, ignorant, passional love, and *vidya-maya*, based on the *love of wisdom*. Furthermore, in terms not of the ancient world but of the medieval one, Dante presents his love for Beatrice as his path to the highest gnostic realization, which is represented by the figure of Beatrice herself as a reflection of the Sophia or Holy Wisdom of God—she who, in the book of Proverbs, describes herself in these terms: 'I love them that love me, and those that seek me early shall find me....But he that sinneth against me wrongeth his own soul: all that hate me love death.' (Prov. 8:17;36).

According to Guénon, 'the way of love is especially appropriate for Kshatriyas, while the way of intelligence is that which is especially suitable for Brahmins.' In terms of the general characters of the castes in question, this is certainly true. But from another perspective, there is a type of love and a type of knowledge proper to each. There is such a thing as a 'jñanic *bhakti*' that discerns within love the laws, forms and secrets proper to love, as well as recognizing love itself as a way of knowing; there is also a 'bhaktic *jñana*' by which Love warms and germinates the seeds of knowledge. The love of the Kshatriya is 'emotive' in the sense that it motivates him to combative, protective and self-sacrificial action, whereas the love of the Brahmin is contemplative rather than passionate; it is like the oil that feeds the clear flame of the Intellect. Once again, it is clear that the Christian mysteries are primarily under the sign of Love—yet no-one would assert that Christianity is primarily a Kshatriya rather than a Brahminical revelation; Christian society has produced both saintly warriors and saintly contemplatives. And the premier Christian *jñani*, Meister Eckhart, spoke of love in these terms, beginning with a quote from St. Augustine: '"What a man loves a man is." If he loves a stone he is a stone; if he loves a man he is that man, if he loves God—nay, I durst not say more; were I to say, he is God, he might stone me. I do but teach you the scriptures.' It is clear that to love a thing is to be united with it, and that perfect union with a thing is also perfect knowledge of it. Or, to approach the matter from the opposite pole, that of knowledge, Jennifer Doane Upton writes: 'The essence of divine knowledge is knowledge of the Good, and to truly understand the Good is to love it.'

Affectivity, which Guénon identifies with life or elemental vitality, is like a fuel that can be burned to empower either the will or the intellect. (By 'intellect' I am referring not to the Transcendent Intellect but to the individual intellect, that faculty of the psyche designed to mirror the Transcendent Intellect in human consciousness, and one that is certainly not limited to rationality alone.) Without emotion the will cannot *will* anything, only impotently wish; but if (at the other extreme) the will is overwhelmed by emotion and therefore passive to it, it is no longer *will*, merely impulse.

Affect is the potency of the will. Speaking in terms of the spiritual Path, without affect the will cannot make good on its intent to concentrate on God; this is why some Sufi orders will make use of poetry and the spiritual concert (*sama*) as well as meditation and *dhikr* (remembrance of God through continuous invocation of His Name). And affect is the potency of the individual intellect as well. If we want to know anything thoroughly—including God, insofar as He can be known (and He will always absolutely transcend whatever we know of Him, no matter how true it is)—we need to be *interested* in that thing. But if we fail to meet the mark in terms of either intent or insight, both will suffer. The highest function of affect, which appears most clearly in the context of the spiritual Path, is to provide energy to will and intellect equally, and thereby reconcile them.

Emotional coldness contracts the perceptions; emotional warmth expands them. *Excessive* warmth or ardor can of course disturb the intellect and unbalance the will, but insufficient warmth will darken the one and paralyze the other. A certain degree of *sang froid* can help pacify an impulsive will and introduce order into a chaotic mind, but too much 'coolness' is as bad as too little; one of the worse errors in spiritual psychology is to simplistically identify frigidity with spiritual detachment. Be that as it may, those whose affections are either too fiery or too frozen will certainly be blind in the area of interpersonal relations, and will therefore become either the victims or the perpetrators of psychological manipulation and injustice. One whose feeling-nature is unsound will be incapable of that aspect of intelligence known as 'consideration', which etymologically denotes either the ability to choose gestures and actions 'with the stars'—that is, in line with the particular qualities of the time—or the related ability to see situations in their fullness, as whole 'constellations' of related factors.

Frithjof Schuon, like Guénon, also sometimes places knowledge higher than love, but he does so from a particular perspective that has little to do with the notion that *thinking* is higher than *feeling*. In *Gnosis, Divine Wisdom*, he says:

> There are various ways of expressing or defining the difference between gnosis and love—but here we wish to consider one criterion only, and it is this: For the 'volitional' or 'affective' man (the *bhakta*), God is 'He' and the *ego* is 'I', whereas for the 'gnostic' or 'intellective' man (the *jñani*), God is 'I'—or 'self'—and the ego is 'he', or 'other'...the majority of men start out from certainty about the *ego* rather than about the Absolute. Most men are individualists and consequently but little suited to make a 'concrete abstraction' out of their empirical 'I', a process which is an intellectual and not a moral one: in other words, few have the gift of impersonal contemplation....

I entirely agree with this the content of passage—except when Schuon says that the process whereby the subjective human psyche becomes objectified before the face of God as Witness, as Absolute 'I', is intellectual but *not* moral. Certainly it is not moral in the sense that it can't be defined as something given by God to the subjective psyche as reward for devotion and obedience, since this could only happen if God were still 'He' and the human psyche still 'I'. But it is most certainly a moral process if by morality we mean the struggle against the passions, the 'war against the soul' (in the words of the Prophet), and if we define passion as the tendency for the Self to become identified with its 'sheathes' (the *koshas* of the Vedanta), with body, feeling, thought, intellect, and bliss—the very process by which God is transformed from 'I' into 'He', and the psycho-physical self from 'he' into 'I'. From the intellectual standpoint, the power which generates this identification is ignorance; from the moral standpoint, both 'volitional' and 'affective', the very same power manifests as passion or vice. The great creator and guardian of the sort of consciousness that takes the psychophysical self as primary and God as merely conjectural is vice in all its forms; to overcome vice, first through active conformity to moral standards and next through overcoming the *division of attention* that the temptation to vice creates, whether or not it is acted upon, is precisely to dis-identify with one's psycho-physical subjectivity, and in so doing deconstruct it; the ultimate end of this process, which is necessarily both intellectual *and* moral, is for the ego to become 'he' once again, and for God once more to be 'I'.

The Devil loves to set up false antitheses, so that damage is done and darkness spread whichever side one takes. And perhaps his favorite antithesis is that between love and knowledge. What could be more in line with his purposes than to pervert affection until it works only to darken the intellect, so that love becomes identified with foolishness in the collective mind, with the result that the most loving among us are repeatedly discounted and wounded until their affections freeze? And what better reveals the quality of satanic pride than that knowledge should be identified with emotional coldness, divine gnosis with social prestige, and intelligence with deceptive cunning, till hard-heartedness itself is seen as a virtue, since if the intelligent are cold, then to become cold must be to become intelligent? In terms of the 'unseen warfare' between the order of Divine Reality and the infernal subversion of that order, some of the most powerful and intelligent of the 'fallen cherubim' would seem to occupy the false division between love and knowledge, and war against all who would bring them closer together, or intuit their intrinsic unity. (One is reminded of the Norse 'rime giants', spirits of abysmal cold, or of the frozen ninth circle of Hell in Dante's *Inferno*, reserved for the betrayers of love.) Rather than our being 'wise as serpents and harmless as doves', these forces would rather see us simultaneously 'harmless as serpents'—brutally cunning—and 'wise as doves'—naïve.

The opposition between knowledge and love is not 'natural',
since to know Divine Reality, the sovereign Good, is necessarily
to love it, and to love it—since love delights to dwell upon its
object—is necessarily to know it. As Maimonides said, 'love is
the highest form of knowledge.' Only in the fallen soul dominated by pride and concupiscence could such an unnatural
opposition exist, since to egotistically indulge in love as a self-
involved emotion is to darken the intellect, and to pridefully
identify with one's indwelling Transcendent Intelligence is to
lay a cold finger on love, both human and Divine. Furthermore,
this opposition between love and knowledge, since it is not in
line with the essential nature of things, is inherently unstable. If
we become comfortable with stupidity we will ultimately lose
the ability to love, since we can't love what we don't want to
know, while if we become comfortable with lovelessness we
will ultimately become stupid, since love is the principle of
relatedness, and we can no longer know what we have refused
to relate to.

In *Spiritual Perspectives and Human Facts*, Schuon says: 'In principle, knowledge is greater than love, but, in fact, in the world, the
relationship is inverse ... and love, will, individual tendency is in
practice more important....' He appears to be wrestling, here,
with formulations inherited from Guénon. I would add, however, that this is correct only if love is identified with 'will, individual tendency'. It is also possible, from a different perspective,
to place love above knowledge, to say that '*investigation*, will, individual tendency' is principially subordinate to a Love that, in the
Divine Essence, is perfectly united with the transcendent Intellect. As Schuon himself says in the same chapter, 'Perfect love is
'luminous' and perfect knowledge is 'hot'.... In God Love is
Light and Light is Love. It is irrelevant to object that one divine
quality is not another, for here it is not a question of qualities—
or 'names'—but of the divine Essence itself.' And: 'The love of
the affective man is that he loves God. The love of the intellectual man is that God loves him; that is to say, he realizes
intellectually—but not simply in a theoretical way—that God is
Love.'

In should be clear at this point that Schuon did not maintain that love is only for 'affective types' or *bhaktas* and knowledge only for 'intellectual types' or *jñanis* in every case and from every perspective. Such a distinction is only valid when our analysis is limited to the requirements of the particular spiritual method under consideration; every complete human being necessarily is, from one perspective, both a *bhakta* and a *jñani*. As Schuon puts it: 'Fundamentally, we would say that where there is Truth there is also Love', and 'The way of love—methodical *bhakti*—presupposes that through it alone we can go toward God; whereas love as such—intrinsic *bhakti*—accompanies the way of knowledge, *jñana*, and is based essentially on our sensitivity to the Divine Beauty.' Through love we 'have knowledge' of the beloved object, and there is no deeper or more complete way of knowing that object as it is, be it a human person or the Divine Personhood itself, and the hidden Ground of which It is the greatest Name.

So we can see that it is both possible and spiritually necessary to integrate spiritual Love into the perspective of divine Gnosis. But what about human love? Of the Sufi formulation of this question, Henry Corbin writes:

> this term *Fedeli d'amore* ... does not apply indiscriminately to the entire community of Sufis. ... In making this distinction we only conform to the indications provided by the great Iranian mystic Ruzbehan Baqli of Shiraz (d. 1209) in his beautiful Persian book entitled *The Jasmine of the Fedeli d'amore*. Ruzbehan distinguished between the pious ascetics, or Sufis, who never encountered the experience of human love, and the *Fedeli d'amore*, for whom the experience of a cult of love dedicated to a beautiful being is a necessary initiation into divine love, from which it is inseparable ... it is a unique initiation, which transfigures *eros* as such, that is, human love for a human creature. (*Creative Imagination in the Sufism of Ibn 'Arabi*, pp 100–102)

From a similar perspective, Frithjof Schuon mentions, as one of the experiences on which a valid spiritual perspective can be founded, 'the experience of earthly love'. In the following passage (from *Esoterism as Principle and as Way*), which is in part a commentary on the *hadith* of Muhammad (peace and blessings be upon him), 'marriage is half the religion', he sets down the principles of true love as a legitimate element of the spiritual Path:

> An indispensable condition for the innocent and natural experience of earthly happiness is the spiritual capacity of finding happiness in God, and the incapacity to enjoy things outside of Him. We cannot validly and persistently love a creature without carrying him within ourselves by virtue of our attachment to the Creator; not that this inward possession must be perfect, but it must at all events be present as am intention which allows us to perfect it.
>
> ....
>
> To be at peace with God is to seek and find our happiness in Him; the creature that He has joined to us must help us to reach this with greater facility or with less difficulty, in accordance with our gifts and with grace, whether merited or unmerited. In saying this we evoke the paradox—or rather the mystery—of attachment with a view to detachment, or of outwardness with a view to inwardness, or again, of form with a view to essence. True love attaches us to a sacramental form while separating us from the world, and it thus rejoins the mystery of exteriorized Revelation with a view to interiorizing Salvation.

True human love is both strictly subordinate to Divine love, and perfectly at one with it. As Jennifer Doane Upton writes: 'Human love in some sense meets its death at the birth of divine love. But in another way, it lives again through that very death, and becomes a symbol of that higher love.

V

Amor was most explicitly developed in the West though the
tradition of romantic or courtly love. This movement flowered
in Christian Europe, particularly southern France, during the
11th century, was an attempt to both spiritualize and humanize
sexual relations. And since aristocratic marriage in that time
and place—romance of course being an aristocratic pastime—
was largely a political arrangement, a relationship of possession
and power, the romantic love movement that grew up in opposition to this impersonality was based on an exultation of adultery over marriage. Marriage was seen as a relationship blessed
not by God but by the Prince of This World, a crass and often
brutal institution for the production of heirs and the consolida-
tion of estates. (It has been seen in this light, with varying
degrees of accuracy, many times since.) Eleanor of Aquitaine
herself was kept prisoner for many years by her husband, King
Henry II of England (she had supported her sons in their rebellion against him, in league with her first husband, King Louis
VII of France); their marriage, like some marriages of the power
elite of today, was a hotbed of political maneuvering and
intrigue. In this social framework, courtly love was in one sense
nothing but a recreational activity for the ruling class, like
today's country club, a chance to play interesting romantic
games and rest up from the work of feudal warfare. But as the
rich have sometimes performed a real cultural service as
patrons of the arts, so the aristocracy of southern France were
patrons of the art of loving; in the refined and 'cavalier' atmosphere of their courts, values of profound import for western
culture were being worked out, both playfully and seriously.
This amalgam of adolescent playfulness and deep truths only
half understood can be seen in the treatise *The Art of Loving Honestly* by Andreas Capellanus (André de Chatelaine), commissioned by Eleanor of Aquitaine, a compendium of the rules and
precedents of the Courts of Love, presided over by her daughter, Marie de Champagne, where lovers' quarrels, love triangles
and other amorous difficulties were settled literally 'in court'. It

could be described as a kind of hybrid between a 'teen romance' novel and a primitive *bhakti* sutra.

Romantic love was a buried foundation—and sometimes an acknowledged pillar—of European culture for almost a thousand years. Though sharing a single milieu with certain heretical movements in its early period (notably the Cathars, or Albigenses), it nonetheless acted as an organic element of Roman Catholic and Anglican Christianity (though not without a degree of tension and ambiguity), as Dante and Shakespeare abundantly prove. It refined the relations between the sexes, and even though it began with an idealization of adultery, it greatly enriched the institution of Christian marriage in the West, by prolonging the spiritual grace of the sacrament of matrimony into the psychic and interpersonal dimensions.

In the mid-twentieth century, writers like Denis de Rougement and even C.S. Lewis to a degree, devalued romantic love, largely in response to a degeneration that progressively transformed it from an aristocratic way of relatedness, which at its idealistic height was a way of self-sacrificial rigor where passion was disciplined by courtesy at one end of the spectrum and the every-present possibility of violent death at the other, into an element of bourgeois mass culture based on the worship of sentimentality; to understand what these writers were reacting against, one has only to remember the 'romantic' motion pictures of the 1940s, as well as the Neo-Pagan instinct-worship of writers like D.H. Lawrence and George Bernard Shaw. The critics had hoped that if Romance were debunked, a more mature and responsible form of love would take its place. But from the perspective of the 21st century we can see that this hope has proved false. Romantic love has been thoroughly discredited, yet its place has been occupied not by a fuller, more human relatedness between the sexes, but by a dizzying fall into emotional numbness, vicious glamour and sexual barbarism.

It is important to make the distinction between the Romance of the medieval 'romances', such as those of Chretien de Troyes, Robert de Boron, Gottfried von Strassburg, Wolfram von Eschenbach and Sir Thomas Malory, and the Romance of the

English and German Romantic Movement of the late 18th and early 19th centuries, whose influence was still strong in the arts until, say, the end of World War I, and in popular culture until the 60's; which had a streak of Promethean individualism (as with Byron and Shelley) missing from Romance in its medieval sense; and whose Lady was as much the world of nature as any human woman, on the theory (I'm thinking particularly of Keats here) that 'girls are nature, so maybe nature is really a girl.' And while there were certain similarities between medieval and modern Romance, medieval Romance can be characterized as 'aristocratic and passionate', while the Romance of the Romantic Movement tended to be a bit more 'democratic and sentimental' (to use the distinction made by W.B. Yeats in *A Vision* between the 'antithetical' and the 'primary'). My emphasis in this essay is more on Romance in the medieval sense of the word; however, I am not using it to refer to the psychology or mores of a defunct medieval social class, much less of any class in existence today, but rather to a particular code of personal and interpersonal honor that is determined by neither birth nor economics, but rather by a sense of the incomparable uniqueness of the human person, as in the saying of Meister Eckhart 'the soul is an aristocrat'. In other words, the light by which a small circle of southern French aristocrats learned to see each other can, in principle though undoubtedly not in collective social reality, shine upon nay one of us, wherever two or more are gathered together in the name of Amor.

Though romantic love grew up in France, many of its greatest literary expressions were German; ultimately it was better served by Teutonic earnestness than by French exquisitry. But, speaking personally, I find myself nearer the mark when I say, simply, that the spirit of Romance is essentially Spanish. Its direct ancestors were the poets of Muslim Spain, and no short poem better renders the heart of romantic passion, in all its aristocratic unsentimentality, than these lines by Abu-l-Hasan ibn al-Qabturnuh (in Lysander Kemp's translation):

I remembered Sulayma when the passion
of battle was as fierce
as the passion of my body when we parted.

I thought I saw, among the lances, the tall
perfection of her body,
and when they bent toward me I embraced them.

This romantic ethos of love and war was elaborated and rar-
efied in France, and raised to its highest spiritual pitch in Ger-
many, in Von Eschenbach's *Parzival*; yet in these six lines are
contained the root of the whole matter—just as, in Ibn al-
'Arabi's phrase, the whole of the coming day is contained in the
first light of its dawn. And even though this is not necessarily a
Sufi poem, the poetry of Muslim Spain was so soaked with spiritual lore (like that of the Elizabethans, notably Donne and
Shakespeare) that it can be read esoterically to refer to the alter-
nation between a state of expansion, produced by an unveiling
of God's Beauty, and one of contraction, under the influence of
God's Majesty—as well as to the phenomenon, well known to
mystics, that a period of spiritual exaltation will often herald a
renewed attack from the *nafs al-ammara* (the lower self), which
can drive one to despair unless it too is recognized as a face of
God: 'Who loves me not in My Wrath will never love Me in My
Mercy.'

The Way of Romantic love requires of a man that he put his
love for his beloved beyond all other earthly values, including
social acceptance and economic security. (It requires the same
thing of a woman but in a different mode, one that has more to
do with endurance and invocation than with exploit—though
women too must be ready to fight, and men to endure). It commands him to go to war against the Dragon of This World, both
within his psyche and in terms of outer circumstances. To love
romantically is to risk all—power, prestige, life itself, the whole
spectrum of worldly, ego-based values—for the sake of love
(though as C.S. Lewis reminds us, when we are tempted to sacrifice other-worldly spiritual values for the sake of romantic love,
then that love has become idolatrous). This is quite literally a

life-and-death struggle that demands total dedication; it is not a path for everyone. A man's love for his Lady is a symbol of his love for God; and since, ultimately, we are nothing other than symbols of That One, there is a sense in which what the Sufis call figurative love, love on the human plane, is a full theophanic manifestation of Divine love. If all sensible and intelligible realities are figures and symbols, then the symbol of the thing, while never ceasing to be a symbol, is necessarily the very presence of the thing itself.

Romance began as a rebellion against the heartless convention of worldly marriage. The heartless conventions of the present day, however, is not marriage, but a profound lovelessness in all areas of life, coupled with a subhuman obsession with the most venomous forms of sexual self-indulgence. Consequently the central act of liberating rebellion against the degenerate social mores is no longer the dangerous, formalized adultery sung by the troubadours, but loving marriage itself. Certainly a marriage of forty years can't be all flamenco; there has to be some coziness too. But the partially-successful attempt of western culture to situate passionate romance within the context of marriage, while in one sense it was nothing but a weak, bourgeois compromise between demands of the ethic of chivalry on he one hand and those of church morality on the other, in another and higher sense was a move to unite Heaven and Earth, to bring back the Golden Age, to make every home and hearth a temple of tantric worship. Because if the relationship between the sexes, in which the power employed by God to create the universe—the power of polarity—reaches its point of highest concentration, is separated from compassionate and self-sacrificial love (which in turn opens the door to the separation of reproduction from sexuality), then the spiritual center from which love radiates into all areas of human life, and even carries over into a fertilizing empathy with the natural world, is destroyed.

VI

In the last few decades the worms of the Yuga have succeeded in devouring the last vestiges of a romantic love grown sentimental, decadent and ripe for destruction. In the wake of this destruction, a vicious sexual glamour and rapaciousness have almost succeeded in becoming the established erotic norm of relatedness between the sexes—except in secret. As sexuality was once hidden by shame, and love cried from the rooftops, now sexuality is openly and shamelessly expressed. What we are now ashamed of is, precisely, love. But without love, sexuality is transformed from a primordial grace and sacrament into a curse, and ultimately loses force. The 'World', the system of collective egotism, is profoundly threatened by the union of love and sexuality that I have called 'Amor', and subverts it whenever possible, either through puritanism or through libertinism, if not by an unholy amalgam of the two. Therefore there must be something in this union that has the power, by the grace of God, to cut the roots of that collective egotism, and which can consequently function as part of a valid spiritual Way.

Romantic love is much more, however, than the union of sexuality and affection, since this union itself requires a sublimation and refinement of soul. Nor is romantic love necessarily young love, nor adulterous love, nor love framed by war, nor even passionate love in the usual sense. Rather, it is that mode of love which is centered on the *vision* of the beloved, by which the alienation between the world of the single Principle and the world of its multiple manifestations is overcome. If love remains imprisoned in the world of the Principle alone, it becomes abstract; if it is identified with the world of outer manifestation alone, it becomes vulgar and dissipated. But when Principle and manifestation are brought into polar, *tantric* relationship, then love reaches the point of both its deepest passion and its greatest renunciation.

Federico García Lorca, in his essay 'The Duende: Theory and Divertissement' (from *The Poet in New York*, translated by Ben Belitt), speaks of this quality of passion as the dark, Divine power that inspires all truly Spanish poetry, music and dance, as well as the art of bullfighting; in line with Spanish folklore he names it the *Duende*, which is sometimes thought of as a kind of elf or household spirit. He writes:

> In all Arabian music, in the dances, songs and elegies of Arabia, the coming of the *Duende* is greeted with fervent cries of *Allah! Allah! God! God!*, so close to the *Ole! Ole!* of our bull rings that who is to say that they are not actually the same; and in all the songs of southern Spain the appearance of the *Duende* is followed by heartfelt expressions of *God alive!*—profound, human, tender, the cry of communion with God through the medium of the five senses....

> ... the *Duende* will not approach at all if he does not see the possibility of violent death, if he is not convinced he will circle death's house....

Duende, in Spanish, is short for *duen de la casa*, 'Lord of the House', which is, in Islam, specifically a title of Allah, as in the Sufi saying attributed to Rabi'a al-Adawiyya, 'first the Lord, then the House'. The House is precisely the Kaaba, draped in black, perpetually circled by pilgrims, dressed in their white funeral shrouds. And so Lorca, eight-hundred years of Muslim Spain still in his blood, reveals to us the essence of Romantic passion as a true name of God, whose human reverberation is *Ishk*—a word that literally denotes the way a vine will hug and wrap itself around a tree, sometimes killing it. It is God's beauty opening, like a wound, to reveal God's Majesty; it is God's Wrath opening, like a rose, to reveal God's Mercy, which eternally rules it.

To have a *vision* of one's human beloved, in either physical presence or absence, is to know him or her as *imaginal* as well as psychical or psychological; it is to see that one as a living symbol as well as an individual, and to know that one's human individuality as a direct emanation from that symbol, which in a mysterious way is both more transcendental and more *personal* than the psycho-social personality. It is to know that one, somehow, as the very image of one's soul, will still granting him his own inviolable uniqueness and solitude.

The Jungians have a lot to say about this kind of romance as a case of the 'projection' of the 'anima' or 'animus' archetype (although, as this type of love continues to fall out of favor, they seem to say less and less). They are right that the experience is an archetypal one; they are also right that the love of another can awaken one to the truth of one's own soul in a way that cannot be limited to one's experience of that other precisely as he or she is, in human terms. But this does not mean that one is simply misperceiving a hidden aspect of one's subjective psyche in the person of another—this is merely the attached, egotistical, 'shadow' side of romantic love. In true romance, each sees in the other the soul they actually and objective share, beyond their separate individualities—over many years of their lives or only for one brief moment—a living symbol which is their common eternal prototype, the particular Name of God from which, over that long life or in that brief moment—they emanate. When the Zoroastrians say that when we die we meet and are united with our eternal counterpart, our *fravashi*; when Swedenborg teaches that a married couple constitute a single angel in eternity; and when Dante encounters Beatrice in Paradise, the same mystery is being alluded to.

If I am only myself, I am sealed in the shell of my ego. If I am only another, then I am, alienated, unrealized; in spiritual terms, if I identify either with God or with myself, I am lost. The mystery is: I am both myself *and* the other, this being the essence of ordinary human romance, of the apparition of the Beloved as an imaginal theophany, and of the *imago dei*, the *atman*, the Absolute Witness itself: Within my soul is Another who is my true Self. Though invisible, He is reflected in the mirror of my Heart; though hidden, that inner Divine Image is reflected in the mirror of the universe. All things I see return Him to my Heart, and my Heart returns Him to the unseen. And ultimately it is only by Him, and *as* Him, that 'I' see.

This inner-and-outer polarity of Lover and Beloved is not duality, but rather the polar manifestation of the Transcendent

Unity of Being. This bi-polar Unity is the origin of the convention found in the Krishna poems of Bengal (as well as in other less elevated forms of erotic play) according to which Krishna and Radha exchange clothes. In the following stanza of a *sahaja* poem by the Bengali poet Vidyapati (translated by Edward C. Dimock and Denise Levertov), Radha addresses Krishna, her beloved:

> *as wing to bird,*
> *water to fish,*
> *life to the living –*
> *so you to me.*
> *but tell me,*
> *Madhava, beloved,*
> *who are you?*
> *who are you really?*
> *Vidyapati says, they are one another*

Jennifer Doane Upton deals with the same theme the following passage from *Dark Way to Paradise*:

In a letter to Charles Williams, Dante scholar Dorothy Sayers complains that, although Beatrice held a high place for Dante, he doesn't seem to occupy such an exalted place for her, at least not in terrestrial existence. Sayers feels that for the sake of justice Dante ought to have had a chance to mean for someone else what Beatrice meant for him. She sees their love as one-sided, and seems not to believe that Dante and Beatrice were ever truly united.

Perhaps, however, Sayers misses the point. At the level of Paradise, where Beatrice takes her proper place, she and Dante are so close to God that the distinction between subject and object begins to disappear. Beatrice drops out of sight in the poem not because Dante has lost touch with her, but because the burden of the subject/object distinction has been removed from them. The great Persian poet Nizami, writing of the lovers Layla and Majnun, tells of how Majnun finds a piece of paper with his name and Layla's written on it. He tears the paper in two and throws away Layla's name, but keeps his own. From that time on, no one can say Majnun's name without including Layla. Likewise, in the last part of the *Paradiso*, Dante no longer speaks of Beatrice because the very possibility of ever being apart from her has disappeared. Not talking with her and not seeing her are no longer able to bring separation.

This mutual mirroring of self and other, which ultimately leads to the transcendence of the subject/object split, mirrors the mystery of God's multiplicity-in-Unity, the overflowing willingness of That One to become apparently other than Himself so as simultaneously be united with Himself in Love and Knowledge. As the Hindus say it, *Sat* (Being) must eternally polarize with *Chit* (Consciousness) so the two may be united in *Ananda* (Bliss). When this mirroring is projected onto the purely psychological level, however, it becomes passional love, attraction-and-repulsion, that negative or egoic side of romance that results in what contemporary psychology calls 'co-dependency'. For God, Self-love is the inherent bliss of His Own Nature; for us it is only narcissism, and results in 'self-ish' love, the 'love' for another falsely considered only as an aspect of one's own identity. In possessive, narcissistic, co-dependent love, the beloved becomes an object of the possessive will rather than the contemplative intellect—as if an eternal, spiritual Unity could be established by the power of personal willfulness, or would ever need to be. The way out of this co-dependency cycle is not through a balance of power, through the establishment of equal and opposite personality-spaces or spheres-of-influence, but in rising to an objective, transcendent spiritual Unity beyond the level of personalities, a Unity that effortlessly allows polarity without either prohibiting or enforcing it.

In light of this we can see how the 'inaccessibility' of the Lady in the courtly romance tradition—which did not necessarily preclude the sexual consummation of the relationship, once the conditions (the 'tasks') were accomplished—had everything to do with the mortification of possessiveness and self-will, and the opening of contemplative Vision. On the other hand, it goes without saying that there can be no Romance without passion. But romantic love is mysteriously capable of being 'passionate, not passional'; the passion of romance, when touched by the Spirit, moves in a self-sacrificial direction rather than a concupiscent one, as when Christ's crucifixion is called his 'passion'. (The word 'passion' denotes *passivity*; it is not something we do or accomplish, but something we undergo, something that requires of us the virtue of *patience*. When vice seizes us, we must actively combat it; when God seizes us, our passivity—not in the sense of sloth or sullen refusal, but in that of intentional and willing receptivity—is our *islam*: 'Not my will but Thine be done.') In this regard, C.S. Lewis said something in his book *Miracles* that is worth quoting:

> we (correctly) deny that God has passions; and with us a love that is not passionate means a love that is something less. But the reason why God has no passions is that passions imply passivity and intermission. The passion of love is something that happens to us, as 'getting wet' happens to a body: and God is exempt from passion in the same way that water is exempt from 'getting wet'. He cannot be affected with love because He *is* love. To imagine that love as something less torrential or less sharp than our own temporary and derivative 'passions' is a most disastrous fantasy.

In genuine romantic love the fire of passion has an alchemical effect; it burns away the dross of egotism and forges the Philosopher's Stone, identified with the Holy Grail on Wolfram Von Eschenbach's *Parzival*, and portrayed by him as Divine Grace working in the realm of human relatedness. And far from limiting this relatedness to the liminal, enchanted realm of the 'love grotto' as found in the Tristan and Isolde romance (de Rougement's *bête noir*), where the passionate couple is isolated from human society, subversive of it, and destined to be destroyed by it, Parzival shows the radiant love of the two principle couples (Parzival and Condwiramurs ['guide of love'], Gawain and Kardeiz) as liberating and redeeming the surrounding society ('all the world loves a lover' as we used to say, but say no longer). And the development of the hero's ability to remain faithful to true love is shown as inseparable from his progressive victory over his own uncouthness, his growing capacity for *courtesy*—a virtue that is as far from the mores of contemporary society as any one could name.

Courtesy should never be regarded as merely the lowest common denominator of civil behavior. A situation that calls for a courteous gesture should be recognized as an opportunity for the exercise of imagination and spiritual intuition, and one that will require as much courage as insight. The saying from the Book of Proverbs, 'where there is no vision the people perish' is nowhere more true than in the area of interpersonal relations. Often the right gesture, made in its own unique and appropriate spiritual moment, will balance, enlighten and purify entire complex situations, and fertilize the matrix of many relationships in a single stroke. Those who are content to perform only the least they imagine to be required of them in this area may progressively lose the ability to meet even the lowest mark of human relatedness.

In this time when all primary human relationships are being systematically destroyed (through, for example, the mechanization of reproduction), many of us have tried to take refuge in God from the death of human love, both through the group-identity of exoteric religion and the struggles and mysteries of the spiritual path. But since the very state of cultural decay that has brought human love to the brink of extinction has also removed the normal exoteric supports of the esoteric Way—like, for example, a spiritually-based social morality that both nourishes and conceals its inner Reality—the esoteric enterprise itself is now more exposed to worldliness and 'spiritual materialism' than perhaps at any time in its history. More and more, the spiritual Path is being sought not as the crown of human life, but as a substitute for it, forgetting that 'none come to the Father' (God's Transcendence) 'but through Me' (God's Humanity). As Frithjof Schuon has written: 'In the case of some people the intention of loving God brings with it an inability to love men; now the second of these destroys the former. In a vulgar soul solicitude for spiritual love and for mortification may bring with it an icy self-centeredness....'

This insidious cold-heartedness was dramatized in a Sufi context by Annemarie Schimmel in her widely-published article 'Eros—Heavenly and not so Heavenly—in Sufi Literature and Life,' when she writes:

> the school of Ibn 'Arabi developed the idea that 'love of women belongs to the perfections of the Gnostics, for it is inherited from the Prophet and is a Divine love.' That is...a foundation for the positive attitude toward sex in later times, perhaps also an excuse for the *all too frequent indulgence in human love*' [italics mine].

We can see quite clearly here a reflection of the contemporary myth, on which various 'popular tantra' movements are based, that sex, since it is elemental, is beyond ego, whereas love, being personal, can only be an expression of ego: the narcissist's version of self-transcendence, as if personal love weren't the one thing that can save sex from falling into heartless cynicism and selfishness. To set the record straight, Ibn al-'Arabi was an illustrious Spanish Sufi, known as al-Shaykh al-Akbar, 'the greatest Sufi shaykh', and was undoubtedly the most profound and prolific metaphysical writer in the history of Sufism, the author of such seminal works as the *Fusus al-Hikam* (the 'bezels of wisdom'), the epitome of his doctrine, and the many-volume *Futuhat al-Makkiyya* ('the Meccan 'openings' or 'revelations'), the most comprehensive known work on the science of *tasawwuf*. As Miguel Asín y Palacios has demonstrated, his writings were an important influence upon Dante's *Divine Comedy*. He also authored the *diwan* mentioned above (a *diwan* is collection of poems) entitled the *Tarjuman al-Ashwaq*—in English, *The Interpreter of Ardent Desires*—which must be named as the pinnacle of love mysticism and theophanic gnosis. This does not mean, however, that Ibn al-'Arabi was some sort of antinomian libertine, as Annemarie Schimmel's characterization might seem to suggest; he was as much an orthodox Muslim and upholder of the *shari'ah* as he was a Sufi (as indeed most Sufis were, until very recently).

Traditional authorities nonetheless maintain that there are valid types of mystical spirituality which bypass human love entirely; and this seems accurate. The *Tao Te Ching* says, for example:

> *Heaven and earth are ruthless;*
> *They see the ten-thousand things as dummies.*
> *The wise are ruthless;*
> *They see the people as dummies.*

Such an attitude is only justified, however, in the case of those who do not involve themselves with the people—seeing that they are nothing but dummies. Those who opt to relate to the human world need to meet the mark of *jen*, the Confucian ideal of 'human-heartedness'. When love withdraws from the human world, hatred immediately occupies it; there is no neutral ground. In these pages I am appealing for the full recognition of the type of mystical spirituality that has no meaning without human love, recognizing it as the privileged and central vessel in which God's Transcendence and Immanence are known as one. Jennifer Doane Upton has said of this tradition:

> In the Christian West, interpersonal relations aren't simply the base from which we pursue our spirituality, as in Islamic countries where such relations are controlled by the *shari'ah*; here they are also the fruit of spiritual maturity, the incomparable way by which the Spirit itself is embodied in our lives.

Certainly every true spirituality requires the sacrifice of attachment; but the same can be said of every loving relationship. How many of us who are committed to one form or another of the spiritual Path habitually mistake coldness for detachment? How many of us try, inappropriately and often unconsciously, to apply the *adab* of the hermitage or the stylite's pillar to human relations, which demand a radically different etiquette? How many of us mistake the emotional numbness and interpersonal alienation enforced by the unconscious social mores, if not simply by the inevitable sufferings of life, for true impassivity? Can we tell the difference between the spiritual virtue of *apatheia* and simple worldly *apathy*? How many of us claim, in the name of either *bhakti* or *jñana*, to have transcended human love, when the truth is that we are simply too cowardly or too arrogant to admit our need for it, and are therefore incapable, until this arrogance and cowardliness are overcome, or remaining faithful to God by means of it? In the words of Frithjof Schuon, 'It is necessary to dig deep into the soil of the soul, through layers of aridity and bitterness, in order to find love and live from it.'

There is indeed a class of mystics who have transcended human love in the love and knowledge of God. But to transcend human love is one thing, and to belittle and betray it quite another. Someone who belittles what he claims to have transcended proves thereby that he is still attached to it. Those who belittle human love are like Eblis (the Muslim Satan) who refused to bow down to Adam, to a lesser being than God, even at God's command. They reject the human form of love because, like Eblis, they fail to realize that all love, in essence, is Divine.

To love what is passing, ephemeral and destined for the grave, to love it with a love that, like all love, is eternal at the core, is to taste the full poignancy of existence amid 'the red dust of this world'. And to ultimately see the human object of one's love as transparent to Love Itself is, in Yeats' words, to 'break the teeth of time'. By means of a profound sacrifice of attachment leading to a radical transmutation of the affections, it is to transform the nostalgia for the past, which is poison, into the nostalgia for Eternity, which is bliss. To live in the intimate knowledge of the inevitable death of one's human beloved is, paradoxically, to see her or him *sub specie aeternitatis*: no longer as an object of love, but as a vision of Love Itself, in which the separation between this world and the next is overcome.

> *Let not my love be call'd idolatry*
> *Nor my beloved as an idol show,*
> *Since all alike my songs and praises be*

To one, of one, still such, and ever so.
Kind is my love to-day, to-morrow kind,
Still constant in a wondrous excellence;
Therefore my verse to constancy confined,
One thing expressing, leaves out difference.
Fair, kind, and true, is all my argument,—
Fair, kind, and true, varying to other words;
And in this change is my invention spent,
Three themes in one, which wondrous scope affords.
Fair, kind, and true have often lived alone,
Which three till now never kept seat in one.

William Shakespeare, Sonnet 105

The Nine
Mirrors of Romance

Romantic love as a strand or emblem of the spiritual Path has, say, eight limbs, which converge upon a ninth as their common center; a number of these have been dealt with above, but they are presented here in a slightly more schematic and *imaginal* way. Some were developed by the troubadours, some by the Sufis, some by the *futuwwah* brotherhoods, some by the *bhakti* poets of India, some by the Fedeli d'Amore, some by esoteric orders of knighthood like the Templars; but despite their uneven appearance in space and time, all are stars in the eternal constellation of Amor. The definitions I've given some of them, particularly those for Chivalry, Adultery, and Gnosticism, are 'sublimated,' expressed in a symbolic manner that is certainly not true to all their social and historical manifestations. Together they make up a 'kshatriya spirituality of the greater *jihad*,' a love-and-war mysticism of the subtle realm. They are:

ONE: The Beloved Hard-to-Attain. A commonplace of Courtly Love is the Lady, aloof and severe, who imposes rigorous tests upon prospective lovers, whose beauty leads knights to risk their lives to win her, and sometimes drives them mad. Like the Grail, she is to be won only by those who combine courage, purity-of-heart and divine sanction. She grants her favors to the one who withstands her tests; all others forfeit their hearts, if not their lives. On the outer, psycho-social level, the Lady's aloofness represents a woman's right to take or reject whom she will—which, paradoxically, must, if it is to be legitimate, be based if upon her understanding that the Love within her is not hers to dispose of according to her whims, but represents a precious treasure—her 'virginity', whether of body or of soul—that is hers only in trust. If no man can claim it without sincerity, sacrifice and mortal risk, neither can she presume to select, on the basis of vanity, lust or the desire for worldly security, who shall win it. Only Love within her can choose the human form who will mirror Him in her eyes.

On the inner, mystical level, the Aloof Beloved is precisely the Transcendence of God, which can only flower into Immanence through the mystical death of the lover in Love itself.

TWO: Courtesy. Courtesy is the virtue which prevents delicacy of feeling and emotional communication from being violated, through frigid indifference, vulgar familiarity, gross possessiveness or seductive manipulation. It forestalls conflict and halts the development of interpersonal injustice. Courtesy is respect for others' boundaries, and our own. It is the understanding that if we fail to give, and receive, the attention required by the shape of the moment, when we make the wrong gesture or omit the right one, we violate the unique humanity of that moment, which will never return to give us a second chance. Courtesy protects human relatedness from being destroyed by the collective egotism of 'the World'.

On the inner level, courtesy is the practice of contemplative objectivity, pure Witness, whereby my act of making a personal gesture, the other's act of receiving it, the other's act of making his or her gesture, and my act of receiving it are viewed from the same standpoint, which is neither in me, nor in the other, nor even in the space between us, but in the mysterious totality of the situation, in the Tao, in God's Will expressed in the shape of this particular moment. As it says in the Noble Qur'an (in the surah *Fusilat,* 53): *We shall show them Our signs on the horizons and in their souls, until it is clear to them that it is the Truth. Doth it not suffice as to thy Lord, that he is Witness over everything?* To apply contemplative objectivity to interpersonal relations prevents us from seeing other people through the obscuring veils of our own subjectivity, and also from being influenced to depart from the objective truth of the situation by other people's subjective reactions. Whoever reaches and unites with this standpoint has become pure mystical detachment.

THREE: Chivalry. Chivalry is the use of overt or implied war-making power to defend what needs and deserves defending. It is based on the recognition that power is not a value in itself except to a barbarian, that only for the defense of values other than war does war have a right to exist—just as, in the traditional Hindu caste system, the *kshatriya* or warrior caste exists to protect the *brahmin* caste, the sacrosanct contemplatives. In terms of western spiritual chivalry, the ideal role of the armed knight is to protect Love from violation by the World, the Flesh and the Devil, and to defend womanhood as Love's symbolic fortress.

Chivalry also relates to the defense of the weak—the socially weak, a duty which has everything to do with romantic love, since the ability to regard, to truly see, those who are repressed and discounted by the World is essential if we are to love without vanity and worldly ambition, since if our choice of a love object is based on the standards of the World, of collective egotism, then our 'love' is a mere ego-investment, a case of self-love in the person of another. This means that, in order to be faithful to true love, one must overcome in oneself the tyrant Vanity, sworn enemy of self-respect. And this inner warfare also has an outer reflection: the war against those social mores, and sometimes against their representatives, that relegate innocence, humility, sincerity and emotional courage to the backwaters of social marginalization.

Integral to chivalry is the virtue of *noblesse oblige*, the knowledge that aristocratic privilege is inseparable from duty, and that this duty involves the recognition and defense of values that occupy areas where the soul of the barbarian, with its worldly cynicism, sees only victims to be exploited, rivals to be defeated, or losers to be ignored. By 'aristocracy' I am not referring to any present social class or bloodline, but to the ability to recognize and respect the inviolable uniqueness of each individual, as in Meister Eckhart's doctrine that 'the soul is an aristocrat'. The knight who possesses *noblesse oblige* knows that 'whatever ye do unto the least of these, my brethren, ye do unto Me.' Chivalry entails the ability to walk what the Sufis call the Path of Blame (*malamah*), to die the death of one's social identity.

Above we recounted the story of 'The Knight of the Cart' from the *Launcelot Romance* of Chretien de Troyes. It is worth telling this story again in the present context, as a western rendition of the Path of Blame as sometimes practiced in traditional Islamic Sufism:

Arthur's queen Guinevere, as we will remember, has been kidnapped by an evil knight, and the Round Table knights have fanned out to rescue her. Hot on her trail, Sir Launcelot encounters a dwarf riding a cart, which '...in those days... served the same purpose as the pillory does now.... Whoever was convicted of any crime was placed upon a cart and dragged through all the streets, and he lost henceforth all his legal rights, and was never afterwards heard, honored or welcomed in any court.' The dwarf tells Launcelot to get in the cart if he wants news of the Queen. He hesitates for two steps, then jumps in. (Gawain, encountering the same dwarf, flatly refuses.) After a series of bloody trials, which include crossing a moat by crawling on his naked hands and feet across a bridge made of the upturned blade of a sword, he succeeds in rescuing Guinevere, whose reaction is: 'You! You hesitated for *two steps* before getting into the cart! What, is your precious honor more important to you than my life?' He shame-facedly admits his fault before her, who, as a representative of the Deity (who else has the right to be so exacting?) will not let him escape 'until he had paid the last farthing.' If Launcelot, like Gawain, had possessed 'normal' worldly vanity, he would never have found a trace of her, since it would have been beneath his 'honor' to listen to the advice of some nameless dwarf—and to the mounted and armed aristocrat, are not all other men necessarily 'dwarves'?

In the inner world, the world of the greater *jihad*, the defense of womanhood is revealed as the struggle, by the spiritually-dedicated individual consciousness (the Good Knight) to protect the 'virginity' of the soul (the Princess or Queen) from rape at the hands of the passions (the Dragon or Evil Knight), and so preserve her primordial receptivity to the Spirit.

FOUR: Adultery. It was a central tenet of Courtly Love that true romance is not possible in the married state, a belief that is now nothing but a cynical cliché. Aristocratic marriage in the 12th century was a political institution, a relationship of power and possession, as it often is today—one blessed, the courtly lovers must have thought, not by God Who is Love, but by the Prince of This World, who is naked power. The critics of Courtly Love who decry such idealized adultery, such as Denis de Rougement, have all Christian values and simple social prudence on their side. Nonetheless the Courtly Love tradition has greatly enriched the institution of marriage in the West. It has spiritualized marriage by humanizing it, by making it personal as well as economic, sexual and social.

To 'adulterate' something is to mix it with something foreign to it, intrinsically incompatible with it. To idealize adultery, however, is not necessarily always to worship sexual chaos; it is also to remind us that, in the area of interpersonal relations, things are not always what they seem. To the degree that society is alienated from God, it will sanction relationships that perpetuate this alienation. In the commandment of Christ, 'whom God has joined together let not man put asunder' is hidden the question: Who exactly has been joined together by God, and who merely by man, by the idolatry of social convention? In these latter days, emotionally and spiritually fertile relationships must be made over the dead body of the prevailing social mores; the one (or several) destined by society to be our mate, the husband or wife of our pride, our greed, our lust, our violence and our stagnation, is not the one destined by God to share in, and help us deepen, our love and knowledge of Him.

In the inner *imaginal* world, where symbols are living beings, the drama of adultery—in terms of the male psyche, that of the beloved woman married to another man who must be outwitted, discredited or killed—will represent either the struggle of the Spirit to free the center of the soul (in Sufi terminology, the *Heart*) from the *nafs al-ammara*, the 'soul commanding to evil', the possessive dragon of the passions, *or* the violation of the holy marriage of Spirit and soul by that very dragon. Whether this inner adultery, the struggle to free the soul from the principle that presently rules it, whatever that principle might be, will serve or violate true love depends entirely upon who presently commands that soul: the Spirit, or the passional self.

Adultery, as well as illicit love between unmarried people (where the cuckolded party will be the parent, not the spouse) is related to secrecy, for obvious reasons. The inner meaning of this secrecy is expressed by Jennifer Doane Upton in these terms:

> The love of God is always secret. For most of us it is so secret that we are not even aware of it. All manifestations that appear around this love are false in a sense, and tend to mis-direct us. To look for the love of God itself within manifest conditions is always to go astray. We spend our time in the world being attracted to this and repulsed by that, and all the while we are blind to this one secret love.

> All stories about secret loves begin to reveal to us the love of God, even though in another sense they may be remote from this love.

The *voyeur* this secret love must be hidden from is the World, the power of collective egotism as expressed not merely in society, but also (or especially!) in one's own psyche. Inner 'spiritual' adultery is in reality the struggle to overturn an intrinsically 'adulterous' union sanctioned by the social ego, and establish a true marriage, which the social ego will then immediately slander as adultery; and in this struggle, even more than in the practice of charity, we must not 'let our right hand (the outer man, the ego) know what our left hand (the inner man) is doing', but keep the secret bedchamber hermetically sealed. Adultery, being a triangle, is based on the number Three, the dynamic number of breaking down and building up—which means that we must accept the struggle to establish the true inner marriage, which is only adultery in the eyes of the world, as a dance, and be willing to move through all the steps of that dance with no guarantees, and when the end is nowhere in sight. Such a dance requires great patience and endurance in the face of excruciating moral and spiritual ambiguities. If we try to 'rectify' (literally 'fourify') the situation too soon with the rational intellect, we will only wound the process, and give aid and comfort to the Enemy; the one thing that will bring us through is faith in, and submission to, the secret will of God operating in the situation, by means of that faith which is 'the presence of things hoped for, the evidence of things not seen.' Only through this kind of faith and endurance will we ultimately be able to 'cuckold the World' and win the true Bride.

FIVE: Youth. The relationship between youth and romance is obvious, since we are normally initiated into romantic love during adolescence. But 'youth' has a much greater potential range of symbolic meanings. The term for chivalry in the Islamic world is *futuwwah* in Arabic and *javanmardi* in Persian, both of which mean something like 'mystical' or 'eternal youth', similar in meaning to the Latin *puer aeternus*. Likewise, our word 'knight' comes from the Old English *cniht* which means 'youth'. 'Eternal youth' can, of course, refer to the young military heroes who come up in each generation, but it can also indicate the quality of freshness or eternal renewal based on the breakthrough of Eternity into passing time. In this it is related to the Islamic doctrine of 'occasionalism', God's continuous instant-by-instant recreation of the universe, according to which one sees every event not as a product of secondary antecedent causes, but as a present act of God. In terms of western chivalry, this is related to the concept of *aventiure* (the French word from which we get our word 'adventure'), which means something like 'casting one's fate to the winds and heroically taking whatever comes as a message from God, a divinely-ordained challenge'; *aventiure* might be called 'the Tao of chivalry'.

At the opposite pole from occasionalism and *aventiure* is the European 'Enlightenment' doctrine of *deism*—the theological basis for scientism—which is the idea that once having created the universe, God ignored it, letting it run ahead on its own momentum, according to pre-established natural law, like a wound-up watch—and there is nothing less romantic than deism. In its denial of Divine Providence and God's love for the world it is the theological expression of all that is hidebound, bigoted, cruel, stupid and mechanistic, of dead matter orbiting through space without love, without intelligence, without God, and of political systems and established moral and social orders just as dead—the whole dreary constellation symbolized by Blake's tyrant god Urizen, symbol of the rational intellect cut off from Divine Truth. Urizen is the *senex*, the Old King, the 'tyrant Holdfast' who sees all change as a threat to his power. 'Eternal youth' in Blake's symbology would then be Orc, the revolutionary breakthrough of Eternity into time, though one destined to decay until it becomes Urizen again—unless, via Los or the Prophetic Imagination, it rises to the level of Urthona ('earth owner') who is not Eternity breaking through into time, but earthly reality fully realized *in* Eternity, beyond the reach of time. If human love falls under the power of 'Urizen' it becomes a struggle to prevent the beloved from changing, a hatred of any expression of new love or new life on his or her part, and so ultimately a kind of murder, whereas 'young' love is capable of seeing the beloved *sub specie aeternitatis*, as totally free to change because, in his or her realized essence, that one is in Eternity already. As Blake says in his famous quatrain:

> *He who binds to himself a joy*
> *Does the winged life destroy*
> *But he who kisses a joy as it flies*
> *Lives in eternity's sun rise*

SIX: Faerie. The atmosphere of western chivalric romance is impregnated with a subtle otherworldliness, inherited from the Celts. This otherworld is neither celestial nor infernal; it is terrestrial, but subtler than the domain of the outer senses: the realm of Faerie. This Celtic 'Land of the Ever-Young' is, in its primordial form, the Terrestrial Paradise as pictured in the final cantos of Dante's *Purgatorio* (though in its fallen aspect it sometimes suggests the Limbo of Dante's *Inferno*). It is what the Muslims call 'the Earth of Hurqalya' or 'the Eighth Clime'; it is Earth as it appears (objectively, though subtly) on the imaginal plane, not the material one. It is peopled by the *Sidhe* of the Irish, the *Jinn* of the Arabs. In its Celtic form it is a land of shimmering beauty and heart-rending nostalgia, but one which, even before the advent of Christianity, had begun to be cut off from the plane of the spiritual archetypes, as evidenced by the fact that it was ruled not by a feminine principle like the Buddhist Prajña-paramita or the Judeo-Christian Holy Wisdom, the principle of the clear contemplation of archetypal realities, but often by a Queen of Faerie who was, to one degree or another, a Goddess of Fate. This Goddess appears in the Grail Romances as the witch Morgan LeFay, a later rendition of Morrigan or Morrigú, the Gaelic goddess of war. The words *fay* and *faerie* are both related to the Latin word for 'fate', *fatum*; thus Morgan LeFay is both 'Morrigan the Fairy' and 'Morrigan the Fate'. When the eternal archetypes are hidden, we can no longer witness the dawning of the Will of God in the eternal present, consequently the forgotten past becomes the seed of the inexorable and mysterious future; Providence, veiled, becomes Fate.

In the romances, the faerie realm, whether directly encountered or simply there in the background like an elusive fragrance, is neutral. It is not Christian; nonetheless it can act as a site-of-manifestation for the Christian revelation—a spiritual possibility most fully developed, perhaps, by the Celtic Christian monks. In response to the grace of the hidden Christ—and to his harrowing of Hades, the realm of the Ancestors—maidens, hermits and armed warriors mysteriously appear to the knight questing through the primeval forest, exactly as the queens and heroes of the *Sidhe* did to his pagan grandfathers, bringing him challenges, messages, tests, appeals, commands: the imaginal forms of God's secret guidance uncloaking themselves, via *aventiure*, on the extreme borders of terrestrial existence.

Romantic love is born and grows up in the Land of the Ever-Young. It is itself the seed of that land (not the other way around) because, as faith in the unseen God is the source of the vision of God in all things ('blessed are they who have not seen, yet have believed'), so the ability to see God manifest in a beloved human form is the source of the vision of the Divine/Human face of the natural world: and this is Eden. The realm of Faerie is therefore nothing less than the Immanence of God as a *human* spiritual potential—though not as an already-given real-ization, because the realm of Faerie can also, too easily, become transformed from the Terrestrial Paradise into Limbo; it can become a dim pantheistic dream that denies the Transcendence of God, and thus also the centrality of Man: and this, precisely is its fall—a fall into a glamorized materialism. But when God is remembered—when, in Celtic Christian terms, Christ redeems the kingdom of Faerie as part of his harrowing of hell—then the subtle realms of material nature respond to that Bridegroom as *Shakti* and Bride. They arise and unite as Holy Wisdom (whose Celtic Christian incarnation is St. Bridget, also known as St. Bride) and regain their human face. The entire natural world responds to the saving reappearance the human form of God's remembrance, Who is Christ, the new Adam, and of Whom each human individual, in the full remembrance of God, is a liv-ing example. Human love manifests Divine Love, and all nature reflects it.

So the love of nature is a natural part of the matrix of Romance, because an openness to the subtle energies of nature, when initiated and directed by God's grace rather than the sor-cerer-ego, refines Eros. (When initiated by the sorcerer-ego, the power complex, it leads to sterility, a state represented Wol-fram's *Parzival* by the castrated magician Clingschor, the enemy of true love, and in the *Perlesvaus* romance, written as a continu-ation of the unfinished *Perceval* of Chetien, by the barren Waste Land.) The refinement and sublimation of these psycho-physical energies is a necessary part of the alchemy of romance; this is the meaning of the Islamic teaching that God gave the Prophet Solomon power over the *Jinn.* According to Henry Corbin's reading of the doctrine of Ibn al-'Arabi,

> For our *shaikh,* King Solomon is . . . the prophet in whom is typified the gift of 'Compassionate Wisdom' (*hikmat rah-maniya,* cf. *Fusus,* ch. XVI), that is, the religion of the *Fedeli d'amore.* Hence the appearance, from the very beginning of the poem [Ibn al-'Arabi's *The Interpreter of Ardent Desires*] with its Koranic reminiscences, of Bilqis, Queen of Saba

[Sheba]... by virtue of her birth, Bilqis is both angel and earthly woman. Thus she is of the same race as Christ... not the Christ of conciliar orthodoxy, but that of the Angel Christology of, or related to, docetic Gnosticism.... (from *Creative Imagination in the Sufism of Ibn 'Arabi*, p326, n16)

In western terms, we would say that Bilqis is a woman of Faerie married to an earthly-yet-divine king, exactly as that king is married to his *realm*: she is his *Shakti*. Solomon and Bilqis: Arthur and Guinevere. Thus the realm of Faerie, via the submission of the subtle erotic energies—the Fairies, the *Jinn*—to the guidance of Spirit, is part of the *tantra* of Romance, a *tantra* whereby the path to the Transpersonal passes not through the realm of impersonal sexual energies, but directly through the unique Personhood of the beloved, placed under the sign of Amor, to whom the energies of impersonal Eros make obeisance. This is one of the many meanings of Christ's saying, 'None come to the Father but through Me.'

SEVEN: Gnosticism. Taken literally, Gnosticism is based on the belief that the universe is a cosmic mistake, created and maintained by tyrannical and deluded false gods: the *archons*, who appear in St. Paul's Gospel to the Ephesians [6:12] as *the rulers of the darkness of this world*: 'We wrestle not against flesh and blood but against principalities, against powers, against the rulers of the darkness of this world, against spiritual wickedness in high places.' As such it is a heresy, a false belief—and one that, since it denies God's Immanence in creation, might be expected to be even more inimical to Romantic Love than orthodox Christianity was. And some of its many manifestations undoubtedly were; certain Gnostic sects practiced such an extreme form of world-denying asceticism that some of their members literally starved themselves to death in hopes of being released forever from the concentric walls (the 'crystalline spheres') of the cosmic prison. One of the enigmas of history, however, is that the most successful Gnostic church of medieval Western Europe, that of the Cathars or Albigenses, who were indeed extreme in their rejection of the world, shared a common culture, centered in southern France, with the more 'worldly' and aristocratic ethos of Courtly Love; nor did these two extremes necessarily and in all respects represent opposing camps. (The idea may have been that a culture that openly allows and even celebrates worldly dissipation must also provide more radical avenues for withdrawal from the world than a culture where a moderate asceticism is more universally enforced—not to mention the fact that no one is attracted to extreme asceticism like the repentant libertine.) And certain Gnostic sects, in their myth of the fallen Sophia redeemed by the Gnostic Savior (often identified with Christ), were closer to a mysticism of Romantic Love than orthodox Christianity; the Gnostic *Gospel of Philip*, for example, identifies the Sophia with Mary Magdalene, and portrays Mary and Jesus as lovers, calling her His 'companion' whom he kissed so often that his other disciples became jealous.

Gnosticism may be a false belief, but to the degree that false beliefs are believed they produce real effects, not only on the psychic plane, but on the physiological, social and environmental ones as well, just as if they were real 'principalities and powers.' In this sense the archons are objectively real; they are real errors, and the Gnostic heresy itself is one of them. But if we understand the doctrines of Gnosticism not as a literal cosmology but as a mythic phenomenology of error, then we are no longer dealing with heresy but with the *science* of heresy: how it develops, how it manifests, how it is overcome. Gnosticism, in this 'sublimated' sense, is precisely the identification and overthrow of idols.

Defined in this way—which is certainly not the way the original Gnostics defined it, and may ultimately be no more than my own particular 'spin' on that tradition—Gnosticism might be called 'the intelligence wing of the greater *jihad*.' Through its methods we can gain insights into the most common stratagems of the commanding *nafs*, or passional soul, as they express themselves both in the individual psyche and in the collective psyche of society. But just as wars are ultimately won by warriors, not spies, so a one-sided development of this kind of 'Gnostic' insight into the shadowlands of spiritual error can paralyze us, and ultimately lead us astray. The greater *jihad* is not won by a Kafkaesque exploration of oppression and illusion, but by the intuition of Divine Reality through collective revelation and individual intellection, and by a deepening submission of the mind, the will and the affections to the Absolute Truth this intuition unveils.

In terms of both Divine Love and human Amor, the war-aim of the greater *jihad* is the triumph of intelligent love over an idolatry of power that is loveless and therefore stupid. On the mythic level this is represented in the Gnostic tradition by the Redeemer's rescue of the fallen Sophia from the power of the evil Demiurge, the chief and original archon, a mythologem close enough to the chivalric motif of the rescue of the Princess from the Dragon by the Good Knight to real a common understanding, if not a common origin. Not for nothing is our only Gnostic holiday, St. Valentine's day ('Valentine' being in all likelihood the Christian Gnostic teacher Valentinus, who almost became pope) dedicated to Amor. Confronted with the established corruption of the social mores in these latter days, the 'spy of the heart' must ask: Which unconscious beliefs stand as enemies to intelligent love? What are their names and how can they be exposed? And which of these enemies do I actually confront in my own life? Which represent mere theoretical distractions, and which stand directly in my Path, such that I simply cannot avoid them, and cannot proceed on my outer or inner Path unless I overcome them? Which of these enemies of love are actually incarnate in outer situations, real situations that I ignore only at my peril, and which of them actually originate in my psyche, such that the true strategy of the greater *jihad* requires that I withdraw these 'projections' from the screen of outer circumstances, and go to battle with them within my own Heart? And how can they be rooted out? It is foolish to believe that all the evil that one sees in the world is actually all in oneself, but it is nonetheless true that the particular objective evils one encounters have a great deal to do with one's actions and character; one is 'tuned' to receive them, as it were. And even if a certain evil is the result of one's own conscious or unconscious actions or attitudes, by the time it appears in outer reality it must be dealt with as an objective factor. Repentance prevents new sins from being committed and new false beliefs from being accepted, but it does not automatically negate the consequences of old ones.

EIGHT: Alchemy. Alchemy is the inner spiritual work that prepares the soul for union with God, both in the purely transcendent dimension, and as reflected in the person of one's human beloved. Integral to the alchemical Great Work is the union of Sulfur and Mercury, the masculine and feminine powers of the soul. Sulfur is the reflection of the active Spirit within the soul, and Mercury the potential receptivity of the soul to that Spirit. This synthesis produces the Androgyne, the restoration of the primordial Adam before Eve was separated. The polar union of masculine and feminine within the soul makes possible the spiritually fertile union of man and woman in the outer world— which means that the man or woman who has realized the Androgyne does not have what we usually think of as an 'androgynous' personality—or a 'macho' or superfeminine one either, for that matter—but rather an integrated masculine personality open to the feminine, or a complete feminine personality open to the masculine. In Jungian language, when the archetype of the Androgyne fails to be realized on its proper level—that of the inner 'syzygy', the vestibule of the Self archetype—it is displaced into the Ego and the Persona, where it produces a formless gender-ambiguity that is not essentially androgynous, but—to use Blake's terminology—'hermaphroditic'. The Androgyne is the polar or tantric synthesis of masculine and feminine powers, positing the transcendence of these opposites on a higher, spiritual level; the Hermaphrodite is a chaotic crushing together of masculine and feminine, ultimately leading to a spiritual state that is lower than sexual polarity, not higher. According to the Qur'an, *surah* 2:187, where the law allowing if not encouraging intercourse between husband and wife on the nights of the Ramadan fast is laid down, *They* [the wives] *are raiment for you and ye* [the husbands] *are raiment for them*, which is another way of saying that the inner essence of the man is feminine, and of the woman, masculine—a traditional source, albeit veiled and allusive, for what we know from Carl Jung as 'anima/animus' psychology. And the fact that this polar sexual quaternity is placed in the context of the 'night' and prohibited during the 'day' shows that it is properly an inner alchemical reality, not an outer psycho-social one.

The inner alchemical work prepares the soul for the romantic encounter, just as true love between a man and a woman, itself a mode of alchemy, empowers and deepens the inner transmutation. This quaternity of inner synthesis coupled with outer relatedness was consciously practiced in some alchemical schools, which held that the transmutation of 'base metal'—the chaotic, hermaphroditic amalgam of Spirit-potential and soul-potential, into 'gold'—the androgynous union of Spirit and soul, *forma* and *materia*, leading to the spiritualization of the body and the embodiment of the Spirit, can only be accomplished through a collaboration between the alchemist and his *soror mystica*, his female assistant or 'mystical sister'. And the greatest literary expression of this 'Christian Tantra' in which inner spiritual development and outer romance, combat and courtesy challenge, purify and complete each other, is Wolfram's *Parzival*. (*Parzival* is revealed as an alchemical romance by the fact that it pictures the Grail not as a cup but as a stone—clearly the Philosopher's Stone—and by an episode near the beginning in which a dwarf named Antenor is thrown into the fire. 'Antenor' is a character from the *Iliad*, but this name also suggests 'athenor', the alchemical vessel in which is synthesized the *homunculus*, a tiny man, partly through the application of fire.)

Romance, which could be defined as Eros alchemically transmuted into Amor, is mysteriously capable of being 'passionate, not passional'. In genuine romantic love the fire of emotional and sexual passion is contained, therefore alchemical, not dissipative, therefore concupiscent. It burns away the dross of attachment and egotism and synthesizes the Holy Grail, the Philosopher's Stone, which is the power of Divine Grace working in the vessel of the spiritual Heart, and thereby transmuting and purifying the field of human relations.

NINE: The Visionary Beloved. The eight limbs of spiritual romance converge upon a common center, that of the visionary or *imaginal* beloved (alluded to in Plato's *Symposium*), as in the Courtly Love convention that love is born in the sight, or enters the heart through the eyes. To have a vision of one's beloved, either in the mind's eye or in the flesh, is to see her or him as a living symbol of the Divinity as well as a human individual, and to know that one's individual humanity as a direct emanation of that symbol, which in a mysterious way is both more transcendent and more personal than the psycho-physical personality. And it is to know the beloved, somehow, as the very image of one's own soul, while at the same time granting that one his or her own inviolable uniqueness and spiritual solitude. Alchemy encounters the Beloved in the subtle world of inner images and energies, the imaginal or *astral* plane, just as faerie-perception (or *etheric sight*) encounters her in another district of essentially the same world, surrounded by that enchanted Land that only appears when the inner eye turns and looks through the outer one. The same order of experiences is encountered as part of the Gnostic espionage, whether this take the form of psycho-social criticism or examination-of-conscience. Courtesy, since it is based on *respect*, which means 'to look again', is the power that allows one to witness the beloved not as an aspect of oneself, through ego-identification, but as Wholly Other, through spiritual objectification. That which I unconsciously take as part of myself is thereby alienated from me, exiled; that which, by the power of respect, I see as wholly and inviolably Other, is revealed thereby as the image of my very Self. Courtesy allows me to know my beloved as a vision, an object not of some dull, half-conscious stare, but of conscious *regard*. When the 'first look', that of the unconsciously possessive ego, is mortified, then the 'second look', that of the contemplative intellect, is born.

Youth, adultery and chivalrous combat also know this imaginal theophany, since these are the circumstances in which the beloved is most likely to be experienced as a vision: in the case of adultery, because of the difficulty the pair have in meeting and the dangers involved; in the case of combat, because the every-present possibility of violent death can, like no other human experience, raise the image of one's beloved to the height of Vision: Facing death, my hunger for life becomes a burning fire, and that fire is She: Dedicated to death, I go to meet it, like a raging ocean with cool peace in its depths—and the roar of those waves is She. When the medieval knight carried an article of his Lady's clothing into battle—just as a modern soldier may carry a picture of his sweetheart—he was courting this very Vision.

And finally, true romantic passion must have at its object 'The Beloved Hard-to-Attain', since this passion is derived from that Name of God in which, like the rose and its thorn, attractive Beauty and inaccessible Majesty unite; and the unattainable beloved is necessarily the imaginal one. In light of this we can see how the inaccessibility of the Lady in the Courtly Love tradition—which did not always preclude the sexual consummation of the relationship, once the conditions (the knight's 'tasks') were fulfilled—had everything to do with the mortification of possessive self-will and the opening of contemplative vision, and acted as a powerful symbolic reflection of the truth that God's grace can never be merited (though if we love Him we will do all we can to merit it), but can only come as a free gift. Only that which is incapable of being possessed by the receiver can be freely and completely given: the aloofness of the beloved *is* her mercy and generosity; the Transcendence of God *is* His Immanence in all things.

To witness the imaginal beloved in the state of dream or waking vision is a call to enter the path of spiritual romance, or the sign that a way-station on that path has been reached, or a challenge and command to leave the station where one has been resting and seek a deeper one, through spiritual labor and struggle. But such a vision is never the culmination of this path. The final end of spiritual romance is 'the spiritualization of the body and the embodiment of the Spirit', whereby we witness our own human beloved, in all her physical glory and bodily lowliness, in all her suffering impermanence and eternal recollection in the mind of God, as the presence of Love Itself.

On Courtesy

The recognition that dignity is not a personal possession but a universal human quality, and the working out of this recognition in interpersonal relations, together constitute the virtue of courtesy. But the particular gesture that will protect, defend or invoke the dignity of another depends both upon the norms of a given culture and on the quality of the time, the Divine imperative hidden in the shape of the moment.

In terms of the virtue of courtesy, our present situation of permanent culture shock presents formidable problems. To the degree that our culture is 'post-modern,' there is no such thing as 'common' courtesy, since the rules of every subculture, immigrant group, corporate entity, human individual, and even every sub-personality within the individual are different, and post-modernism allows no 'overarching paradigm' to intervene in order to unite them. To 'celebrate diversity'—an admirable goal in itself—is inseparable in fact from the parallel social command to 'destroy unity'; consequently we are always in danger of unintentionally insulting one another. And to the degree that we become insensitive to other people's feelings because we don't understand their emotional language, we usually develop a corresponding oversensitivity to insult when it comes to our own feelings. This, as anyone can see, is a perfect recipe for the kind of violence we are presently experiencing in our streets, our classrooms and our homes.

It was common for my (Baby Boom) generation to put down courtesy as 'just a lot of rules'. And the use of formal etiquette by our parents' generation as a way of shaming us—which, of course, is the antithesis of real courtesy—was a contributing factor in our desire to live spontaneous lives with no objective standards. But what could be more anxiety-producing, finally, than a life without any objective rules of interpersonal conduct? You never know, under such circumstances, when something you say or do will hurt someone and turn them into an insidious poisoner or a savage beast. And you are equally in the dark as to whether an insult you feel is deliberately intended, a product of innocent insensitivity, or a figment of your own imagination. (Clearly I am painting an exaggerated picture her, but you get the idea.) To the degree that we have achieved our ideal of a life without objective standards of courtesy, we live in a hell of social paranoia, where the strategic choices seem to be to overwhelm others with our charm, intimidate them with our potential violence, or numb out to them and withdraw into our shell. A social life without the virtue of courtesy, then, is a life in which—to repeat Sartre's phrase—'hell is other people,' in which anyone may severely wound or seriously drain us without warning, and where the only way to avoid these dangers and still relate to others seems to be to totally identify and blend with them, the strategy that has come to be known as 'co-dependency'.

But relationships based on mutual identification are more draining and wounding that any other kind. If we can't tell another person apart from ourselves, then any act on his or her part that is not in line with our desires or expectations—either stated, unvoiced or unconscious—is felt as rebellion or betrayal. In an attempt to shelter ourselves from such felt betrayal, we enter into what we hope will be betrayal-proof relationships, ones in which a dissonance of wills between self and other can supposedly never arise. We seek out people we think we can totally control, people willing to totally control us, or herdlike groups into which we can happily dissolve our will into the group will. But to appoint someone to tyrannize over you is in effect to make that person your slave, since you are placing on her or him the entire burden of your life decisions, which will weaken that person to the point where you can subtly become the enslaver. Likewise, to make someone a slave is to put that person into a position by which he or she can enslave you by the same process. And to submerge your identity in a herdlike group is to contribute to a system in which the development of slaves and tyrants becomes inevitable, since the suppression of

individual uniqueness, which is the manifestation of the Absolute in the relative world, can only result in the development of
the social form known as the *pecking order*. Wherever uniqueness
is suppressed, self-definition becomes necessary, and the only
form of self-definition possible under such circumstances is
comparison of oneself with others on a scale of knowledge or
charm or power. This is precisely what Shakespeare was referring to when he said 'Comparisons are odious'.

Courtesy, on the other hand, has to do with respect for
uniqueness, with maintaining boundaries, with the virtue of
discretion—which is why, when my generation threw courtesy
out the window, so many of us ended up with boundary-prob-
lems: emotionally isolated, in co-dependent relationships, or as
members of cults.

The word *courtesy* means 'the way things are done at the royal
court.' Historically speaking, courtesy has been a more or less
aristocratic virtue, a code of conduct applicable to those who
are individuals in their own (socio-economic) right—at least
when contrasted with the more democratic virtues of team
spirit or group identification; consequently courtesy has always
been related to the concept of honor. (Nonetheless in various
traditional societies, such as many tribal groups, or in traditional
Islam, the virtue of 'aristocratic' honor is, or was, widely distrib-
uted throughout society at large, irrespective of socio-economic
position.) And while honor at its best is faithfulness to one's
principles, in another and lower sense—undoubtedly, the most
dominant one historically—is has in effect been the worship of
one's reputation as intrinsically more valuable than one's life. In
times of chivalry, aristocrats and their retainers alone had the
right to keep and bear arms, and any insult to one's honor or
reputation demanded satisfaction in combat. So it was incumbent on the aristocrat be at least courteous enough not to insult
another *intentionally*—otherwise he would have a short and violent life. This code of behavior is one reason why aristocratic
classes in general have developed both the art of courtesy and
that of deliberate insult to a high degree.

But as a spiritual virtue, courtesy is something else. The first step in moving aristocratic 'courtesy' in the direction of spiritual courtesy is the concept of *noblesse oblige*, the doctrine that someone in a high social station must pay, as it were, for his or her privilege by extending courtesy beyond the bounds of class, as far as the least privileged of his or her countrymen. Both Muhammad, insofar as he was a prophet, and Jesus, insofar as He was a King, possessed this virtue in its most pristine form. When Jesus consorted with the most despised members of Jewish society, when He said 'whatever ye do unto the least of these, my brethren, ye do unto Me,' he was manifesting this 'obligation of nobility'.

The virtue of *noblesse oblige* is essential to the code of chivalry, since for the aristocratic man, which meant the armed man, to extend courtesy to 'the least of these' sometimes entailed ultimately defending them with force of arms. I am not saying, of course, that this was the prime function of the aristocrat, who usually spent more of his time oppressing the weak than defending them, but it was the explicit code and conscious ideal of certain military orders of chivalry, such as the Templars (who, nonetheless, were widely hated at one point for their arrogance). And this military expression of noblesse oblige undoubtedly worked to prevent it from falling into its shadow side, which is condescension. It's difficult to be condescending when one is risking one's life.

As American society continues its descent into emotional coarseness and physical violence, more and more of us are forced to become hustlers—economically, socially and interpersonally. We learn to sell ourselves, to compete for attention in the same way that we hustle for our daily bread. Consequently only the most obvious expressions of personality tend to remain socially acceptable, or even visible. But just as the viability of the ecosystem depends upon many small, subtle relationships, on a rich variety of species as opposed to a few dominant and/or exploitable ones, on the fertile tenderness of the embryonic beginnings of things, so any viable society is necessarily based on a subtle web of primary human relationships, on a wide spectrum of socially acceptable feeling tones and ways of being together. But it is this very sense of emotional diversity that contemporary American society is losing fast. And once collective consciousness of a particular form of feeling-relatedness is lost, it is transformed from a conscious expression of our humanity into an unconscious complex, a possessing ghost. If we have never experienced the particular feeling-tone of close male companionship, for example, we may interpret any such incipient feeling as a homosexual urge, and either suppress it or act it out. If we have never felt the tone of parental love, we may interpret any warm feelings we have for a child as sexual as well. The Sanskrit language has dozens of words to describe the various feeling-tones we cover with the single word *love*. And it may well be that the impoverishment of our erotic and emotional imagination and language is the real root of our obsession with sex, as if any love that does not include sexual expression is not really love. As the energy of wounded Eros withdraws from our barbarous architecture and devastated environment, it becomes concentrated in the moment of the sexual act itself—but this is a burden that the simple act of sex, no matter how elaborately we try to enhance it and embellish it as 'sacred sexuality', simply cannot support. And it is to some degree the pressure we put on sex to stand for a whole lost world of life forms and subtle emotional responses that contaminates our sex lives with the impersonal coldness and demonic violence we now see manifest.

In such a toxic psychic milieu, the struggle to preserve, defend and enhance emotional subtlety becomes, literally, a matter of life and death. The interpersonal equivalent of 'Who cares about some rare wetlands mouse? We need a dam,' or 'Who cares about the spotted owl? We need lumber,' is: 'Who cares about a social non-entity who isn't fascinating, glorious or powerful? We need relief from stress, a sense of physical security, and emotional and sexual excitement *now*.' The result of this addiction to emotional coarseness is that those individuals and values necessary for the continued viability of human social life are weeded out, by a kind of survival of the unfittest, until only the most destructive individuals and tendencies remain standing in the arena.

How can we work against this? One way, though difficult, is comparatively simple. We need to train ourselves to redistribute the available attention. In an immature and emotionally coarse group dynamic, the few 'interesting' individuals will monopolize all the attention. Now it will always be normal for certain members of a group to remain a little more aloof and less demonstrative, while certain other will be more expressive; and it is our duty to respect someone's need to be in but not of the group process, as well as the need (within limits) for self-expression. But as soon as vanity enters the picture—vanity being the tendency to give attention only to those with whom one has identified one's ego, while others present fall into the frigid and unconscious shadow of that ego—then a condition of oppression exists, and vigorous and chivalrous action against such oppression is demanded. Such action can be divided into four gestures: (1) To withdraw excess attention from anyone you are fascinated with; (2) To deflect excess attention that is being directed toward you for the same reason; (3) To pay attention to whoever is being cut out of the group awareness through glamour and vanity, while taking care not to intrude upon someone's privacy; (4) To receive the attention and expression of those who have been suppressed by the group dynamic, and allow it to affect you on the deepest level. Though these four gestures can be viewed as no more than common courtesy, in situations of social discourtesy and oppression they can have a revolutionary edge to them, a silent, but formidable and blade-like energy. Any group will automatically repress and ignore those individuals and values that are threatening to the group ego, even if the threat is no more than the first intimations of the disturbing awareness, by the perpetrators, that people's sensitivities are being trampled upon. And the forcible return to consciousness of repressed material always entails pain on the part of the repressors, and often also of the repressed. Without a willingness to endure such suffering our habitual unconscious can never be overcome, nor will Divine Love ever show his face in our circle.

This is one way in which courtesy is chivalrously extended to the weak and oppressed in social situations. But there is another mode of courtesy that needs to be mentioned, and that is the warrior courtesy that we are required to extend to one who is both an equal and an opponent. The following are twelve rules for any courteous and strategically effective encounter with such an opponent:

(1) Always respect your opponent. Know that your opponent is host to the *imago dei* just as you are, though opposed to you in a given situation.

(2) To respect your opponent is to see him. If you don't see your opponent, he will cut you.

(3) To respect your opponent is to witness his true gesture.

(4) If you become angry with your opponent, he will cut you.

5) If you flee from your opponent, he will cut you.

(6) If you pity your opponent, he will cut you. (Blake: 'Pity divides the soul.')

(7) If you belittle your opponent, he will cut you.

(8) If you try to ward your opponent off (repress him), he will cut you.

(9) If you identify with your opponent (confuse yourself with him), he will cut you.

(10) If you identify your opponent in any way with your ego, if you attach to your reactions to him or his reactions to you, he will cut you.

(11) In the final analysis, the only way to defeat your opponent is to transcend your ego. As soon as the ego dies, God takes the field. As soon as God takes the field, no opponent remains.

(12) If you want to disarm your opponent, receive his gift.

The essence of courtesy is respect for another's uniqueness, for the image of God within him—a respect that can only be based on an equal respect for the image of God within oneself. Our *fitrah*, our primordial humanity, is our deepest possible point of contact with the unknowable Divine Essence; we must take care that our humility before that humanity as it appears in another does not become, under the dehumanizing influence of the unconscious social mores, a humiliation of that same humanity as in appears in ourselves; no-one lacking in self-respect can ever truly respect another.

The ability to stand in a conscious, polar relationship to the Divine in oneself is the root of the analogous ability to stand in the same sort of relationship with another—and this is the essence of courtesy. Martin Buber, in his classic work *I and Thou*, makes a distinction between relationships of identification, which he called 'I/It' relationships, and polar relationships, which he designated as 'I/Thou'. According to Buber, we try to overcome alienation, to heal the split between subject and object, by dropping one of the terms, by falsely imagining either that there is no real universe or that there is no real self. Either we devour the other or let it devour us, but we never really meet it until the alienated I/It relationship (which is really an It/It relationship) rises to become an authentic relationship of I/Thou.

A relationship of identification is nothing but possessiveness and egotism. But when the conscious, polar relationship—the *tantric* relationship—between authentic self and authentic other is resolved, the result on the human level is emotional fertility, and on the Divine level, mystical Union with God. Union with God requires courtesy above all, since if we take God for granted, or try to take Him by storm, we are firmly repulsed. But if we wait on Him with patience, courage and humility, and in constant remembrance, then the next move is His—and as soon as God as much as lifts His finger, the prize is won.

So our society is descending into barbarism; can anything be done about it? Kung-fu Tzu (Confucius) also faced a Chinese society descending into social and political barbarism; his 'idealistic' and 'impractical' response was to try and re-introduce the traditional mores of 'gentlemanly' conduct. He was apparently a total failure in this attempt. Chuang Tzu tells the story of his self-imposed mission to 'civilize' the warlord Robber Chih—who (not surprisingly) simply held him for ransom until his friends bailed him out. All he accomplished in his own lifetime was to found a small group of scholars dedicated to his ideas.

After their master's death, however, this tiny band became the seed of a humane culture that spread over the centuries throughout the Middle Kingdom, infusing every level of Chinese society with essentially Confucian ideals. The central virtues taught by Confucius were essentially those related to *courtesy* in the highest, widest and deepest sense of that word, applicable to relations between family members, community groups, social classes, and even nations. They are as follows:

(1) *Compassion* or 'human-heartedness', conceived of as the natural way human beings relate to one another according to the 'golden rule'.

(2) *Filial Piety*—the willingness to support, put up with, and sometimes even sacrifice oneself for one's parents, especially aged parents.

(3) *Righteousness* includes both the ability to consider the greatest good for the greatest number, and the allied ability to protect oneself by not stirring up unnecessary conflict. Righteousness (as well as *Propriety*, below) might be defined as 'human-heartedness in action'.

(4) *Propriety* is courtesy and inter-personal sensitivity, as well as responsiveness to the specific needs of the present moment—as is specifically taught, for example, by the *I Ching*.

(5) *Loyalty* simply means the kind of loyalty to one's family, community or nation that motivates one to work or sacrifice on their behalf.

(6) *Reciprocity* is inter-personal justice, observance of the mores in terms of what one owed to others, and what one has a right to expect from others, on all levels.

If such virtues are not being expressed in society as a whole, it will still be possible for a person to base his or her character and social relations on the work of developing and manifesting them. And the root of the whole matter is *human-heartedness* or *jen. Jen* is the origin of all courtesy, and reveals it to be a virtue that ultimately springs from a level deeper than any formal social rules, the level of the primordial human nature that the

Muslims call *al-fitra*. Whoever does not *claim* his own existence, whoever does not *identify with* himself or *own* himself, will see himself (or herself)—in the manner of a traditional Chinese painting—as nothing but one more little figure in the human landscape: objective, as everyone else is, to the Absolute Witness. Each human individual is unique, just as each moment is unique; to fail to recognize this to lose the ability to give persons and moments their due, thereby betraying the virtue of courtesy. But it is equally true that the One who looks out through the eyes of every unique individual is the same in each: the Absolute Witness. Without this recognition, true courtesy is impossible. Only the person who recognizes that there is no division in essence between the universal One and Its many unique instances may claim to have brought the virtue of courtesy to perfection.

Chivalry,
East and West

Its Historical Corruption
and Eternal Essence

I: Introduction

As I have already pointed out, it is certainly not news that the culture of the West is profoundly degenerate, that it is in the midst of a headlong fall into technological, economic, political and moral barbarism. The Abu Ghraib prisoner abuse scandal, by which the United States abused itself every bit as much as its unfortunate victims, covering itself with an ineradicable and public shame, may stand as a convenient emblem of this terminal corruption, which touches every one of us, both in grossly obvious ways and in other ways that are harder to discern and define. In this essay I intend to shine what light I can on some of the subtler forms of this disease, particularly the corruption of the virtues of *courtesy* and *chivalry*, of all that used to constitute the accepted conduct of those quaint, almost mythological beings known as 'gentlemen' and 'ladies'—people who were, in many cases, our own parents and grandparents. In particular, I want to say something about what may happen when an eastern code of conduct, taken out of its cultural context, encounters a Western culture where the virtues of courtesy and refinement of feeling have not only decayed, but actually inverted, where cruelty and crudity, at least in certain circles, have become occasions for pride, not shame.

To say the very least, the chivalry and gentlemanly conduct that some of our forebears took for granted as decent adult behavior is no longer in force. The West (and it is not alone in this) is sinking into a moral barbarism perhaps unparalleled in the history of the world. And this sort of degeneracy in Western mores is what Asiatic immigrants to the West cannot easily understand. How could they, when we ourselves, by and large, do not see or understand what is happening us, when we can't effectively remember how people treated each other, or were supposed to treat each other, even thirty years ago?

Today's world is a battlefield where spiritual traditions and cultural norms from all over the globe are being thrown together by inexorable historical forces, informing and deceiving each other, enriching and wounding each other. Few if any of the 'observers', 'proponents' or 'victims' of these forced exchanges of cultural influence are aware of more than a small fraction of the transformation or damage they represent, simply because full objectivity is nearly impossible in the absence of a single, stable world-view upon which to base such objectivity. We are on Matthew Arnold's 'Dover Beach', *where ignorant armies clash by night*. We are all winging it, treading water, doing our best to ignore the daily blows, or so obsessed with figuring out what is happening that we lose what little psychic balance we may once have possessed. And not only does culture clash with culture; the seemingly inviolable norms of past traditions also clash with the implacable and evanescent norms of the 'present day', norms which change so rapidly and unpredictably that the use of the word 'norm' to describe them has become seriously ironic. And behind the war of past against present lurks the war of past against opposing past. It is as if even the ancestors were at war with each other, giving further meaning to the dictum of Marxist critic Walter Benjamin that 'the dead are not safe'.

In my treatment the chivalric traditions of the East and the West, and their degeneration, I will concentrate—largely, though not exclusively—on what until recently has been considered properly sensitive and decent conduct between the sexes, as well as contemporary society's all-but-universal betrayal of these standards. And within these bounds I will pinpoint, along with other aspects of our contemporary moral decay, a particular problem of our 'pluralistic' society that I have named *spiritual misogyny*. But before I do this, I need to say more about what chivalry is in itself—about its intrinsic nature as a spiritual virtue that cannot be touched by the corruption of time, since it is a reflection within the human soul of an eternal Name of God.

II: Muslim vs. Christian Chivalry

The Arabic word *futuwwah* is most often translated by the English word 'chivalry'. *Futuwwah* (and its Persian equivalent, *javanmardi*) denotes the quality of the *fata* or 'eternal youth' (*javanmard* in Persian), the ideal model of young manhood: brave, courteous, heroically self-sacrificing, and charismatic (in the spiritual not the worldly sense of that term, *inshallah*)—qualities that will immediately suggest, to any Muslim, the character of the Imam 'Ali, the purest exemplar of Muslim chivalry. The power of this archetype in the Islamic world is demonstrated by the fact that God Himself appeared in imaginal form to Ibn al-'Arabi at the Kaaba in the form of a *fata*.

The English word 'chivalry', however, carries a nuance that *futuwwah* does not share. 'Chivalry' literally means 'having to do with horses'—in other words, with mounted aristocrats, and war as fought by aristocrats. The code of Western chivalry shares many ideal virtues with *futuwwah*; both denote a quality of what we would call *knightliness*—a word that, like *futuwwah*, has to do with youth: 'knight' literally means 'boy' or 'young man'.

The major difference between the eastern concept of chivalry, perhaps best expressed in *The Way of Sufi Chivalry* by Ibn al-Husayn al-Sulaymi, and that of Western Europe is that the ideals of chivalry were progressively identified, in the Middle Ages and later, with those of *romance*; thus the knight became the ideal lover as well as the ideal warrior. Most or all of the elements that comprised the ethos of Western chivalry were present in Islam as well, but they remained more-or-less separate streams. The *udhri* poets of the early days of Islam celebrated unrequited platonic love in terms almost identical to those of the later troubadours of Europe, and romances such as *Layla and Majnun* by Nizami and *Yusuf and Zuleikha* by Jami have much in common with Western romances of doomed yet *mysteriously requited* love, like that of Tristan and Isolde, or the story of the disastrous adultery of Launcelot and Guinevere from the Arthurian cycle. Western chivalry, then, might be roughly defined (in Islamic terms) as *futuwwah* plus the *udhri* ethos plus certain elements of Arabo-Persian romance, all of which, in their inner meaning at least, are understood to have a deep spiritual significance. And in both East and West, chivalry has been much more than simply a literary convention—which is all that it now seems to be, in its decadence. In both Muslim and Christian lands it represented a necessary and defining element in the character of any man or woman who deserved to be called a 'gentleman' or a 'lady', terms which originally denoted aristocratic birth, were later applied to 'well-bred' members of the middle classes as well, and have since (in the space of my own lifetime) gone out of use.

Chivalry is based on a recognition that the dignity of the human state is not limited to oneself, nor to those who are great or fascinating or powerful in a worldly sense. In Islamic terms, we can say that every human being is an expression of the human essence, the *fitrah*; therefore every human being is, potentially, *khalifa*, God's fully-empowered representative in this world, whether or not he or she is faithful to this trust. To practice chivalry is to do justice, and the highest level of justice requires that we extend it without demanding it, recognizing that our own demands—on our friends, our family, our neighbors, our employer, or our government—might themselves be the major imbalance in our immediate situation, and the only one we really have the power to put right. (In order to make this kind of sacrifice, however, we must first be sure that we are not relinquishing our rights out of simple cowardice; the one who fears to assert his own rights will probably also lack the courage to defend other people's rights, or do them justice when times get hard.) A pertinent story is told of Dhu l'Nun, the great Egyptian

Sufi. There was a drought in Egypt, and the people implored him to pray to God for rain. He did so, and during his prayer God informed him that he himself was the source of the drought. So he left Egypt, and the rain came.

In the words of Hazrat 'Ali, 'the best form of justice is succoring the oppressed'—not only the politically oppressed, but also those who are made outcasts, ignored or ridiculed by society. Injustice is basically imbalance—and one of the great imbalances in worldly society is *imbalance of attention*. Those who are powerful or charismatic command all the attention, while those who are not, no matter how sincere or virtuous they may be, are deprived of it. Attention is like food: to crave it is a form of gluttony, but to be severely deprived of it is a kind of starvation. And while it is the better part of virtue not to *demand* attention, the virtue of justice requires that we *give* everyone the attention he or she needs—no more, but certainly no less. In a social situation where courtesy has degenerated, and which has therefore become unjust, sometimes strong intervention is needed to re-establish the balance. The following story is told of one such intervention:

> Among the people of Medina there was a particularly ugly little man called Zahir. The Prophet was fond of him, and seeing him one day in the market, came up behind him and slipped his arms around his waist. Turning in surprise, Zahir shouted 'Who's this?' and then, seeing who it was, leaned back against the Prophet's chest. The Prophet called out: 'Who will buy this slave from me?' 'Alas,' said Zahir, 'you will find me worthless goods, I swear by Allah.' 'But in the sight of Allah you are by no means worthless,' said the Prophet. (Charles Le Gai Eaton, *Islam and the Destiny of Man*, p121, n2)

In Islamic terms, this is an example of true *futuwwah*, but it is not an example of Western chivalry, which is inseparable from an idealized romantic love. And perhaps the greatest barrier to a mutual understanding between West and East of how our respective ideas of chivalry differ, and also of what they have in common, is that chivalry is dying in the Muslim lands, while in 'post-Christian' Europe and America, it is already dead. Consequently we are hard-pressed to draw examples of either true Islamic *futuwwah* or true Western chivalry from our own experience, but must first resort to obscure medieval literature, and only then ask whether these *romances* can still illuminate examples of chivalrous behavior in our contemporary world. And if the answer is largely 'no,' then the next question is: can cultural values that have been exiled from collective society find refuge in smaller circles of people dedicated to the spiritual life? This remains to be seen.

In both dar al-Islam and Christian Europe, organized chivalry first assumed the form of the military order. The first 'chartered' Muslim order of chivalry, founded by the caliph al-Nasir ad-Din Allah (reigned 1180–1225), was given its rule by the famous Sufi saint Shihab al-Din al-Suhrawardi (d. 1234), just as the rule of the Knights Templars was composed by St. Bernard of Clairvaux. After this 'courtly' *futuwwah* went into decline, some of its rituals and part of its role were picked up by the 'popular' *futuwwah* brotherhoods who were for the most part connected with artisans' guilds, just as Templar influences, after the suppression of the Order, later turned up in Freemasonry. Even though chivalry progressively lost its strictly military function, its influence on the social mores continued in other ways. Yet the military origins of chivalry, its quality of combat, no matter how bloodless or sublimated, still remained as part of its essential spirit.

I once asked an Iranian *darvish* to give me an idea of the spirit of *futuwwah* (which was an important historical influence on many Sufi orders). He answered: 'The best example of a Western *fata* I can think of is the Kris Kringle character from the Christmas movie *Miracle on 34th Street*, the old black-and-white version.' One character in that motion picture is a young man, decent and sincere, but also shy, overweight and unsure of himself. A cruel psychiatrist tries to convince him that he is mentally ill, and since he has little confidence in himself, he accepts that judgment. But Kris Kringle—a department-store Santa Claus who turns out to be the *real* Santa Claus (or at least believes he is), defends the young man against the psychiatrist by giving him a good tongue-lashing and a bop on the head—after which Kris Kringle himself is accused of mental illness—after all, he *does* have the delusion that he is Santa Claus. Kris ultimately triumphs at his sanity trial, but before that happens he succeeds in defending the young man oppressed by the evil psychiatrist by *taking the accusation of insanity upon himself*, after which the psychiatrist forgets about tormenting the young man and goes after Kris instead. This is directly in line with an important element of Sufi chivalry: the willingness to play the scapegoat to save others—a form of self-effacement that will immediately suggest, to any Christian, the redemptive self-sacrifice of Jesus ('Kris' clearly being an allegory of Christ). This seeking out the role of social scapegoat is the basis of the spiritual function, within Islam, of the *malamatiyya*, the 'People of Blame', who are strictly analogous to the 'Fools for Christ' within Eastern Orthodox Christianity. (Perhaps the martyrdom of al-Hallaj, who seems to have deliberately sought out social disgrace, may ultimately have had a similar function of protecting those Sufis in whose cause he sacrificed his life, by virtue of the remorse that affected large sections of Muslim society after his martyrdom. As Jesus said, 'no greater love a man hath, than that he lay down his life for his friends.')

III: Muslim and Christian Chivalry vs. Spiritual Misogyny

The quality of heroic self-sacrifice to protect others from physical danger or social oppression is immediately recognizable, in both East and West. But when the element of *romance* enters the picture, things get more complicated. Annemarie Schimmel claims that even Jalaluddin Rumi, one of the greatest of Sufi shaykhs, known as the 'Pole of Love' (just as Ibn al-'Arabi is called the 'Pole of Knowledge'), once characterized married life as (in Dr. Schimmel's words) 'an educational process in which the man wipes off his impurities onto the woman' (*Deciphering the Signs of God: A Phenomenological Approach to Islam*, SUNY Press,

1994; p200). Perhaps in the context of his place and time this meant—or at least meant to him—that it was the men who were impure, and the women who, by their intrinsic purity, could help purify their menfolk. But, to the western ear at least, such a statement is truly foul; there is nothing chivalrous, really—in either Christian or Muslim terms, I'm sure—in comparing women (in effect) to cleaning rags. The misogynous statements by many recognized Christian saints—such as Augustine, who denied that women as 'helpmeets', though not as human beings, are made in the image of God—are just as foul, if not more so.

On the other hand, Rumi exhibited true chivalry in defending his daughter-in-law Fatima against her husband, Sultan Walad. According to *The Quatrains of Rumi: Ruba'iyat-e Jalaluddin Muhammad Balkhi-Rumi*, translated by Ibrahim W. Gamard and A. G. Rawan Farhadi (Dari Books, 2008):

> He [Rumi] wrote that her sorrows were his sorrows, as well as her concerns. He expressed the highest respect for her (deceased) father, saying that he was so indebted to him that he was unable to pay for it. 'Only the treasury of God Most High will be able to pay the gratitude for it.' He told her that his expectation from her was that she should not conceal any suffering, so that he could help her as much as possible. He said that if his son continued to trouble her, he would detach his own heart from him, not answer greetings from him, and not wish attendance at his own funeral from him—or from any others who supported him against her.

But no less a figure than 'Ali ibn Abi Talib offered a faint but unmistakable slight to the Prophet's wife A'isha on the occasion of 'the affair of the necklace', an event that might well have been one of the factors behind the later split between the Sunnis and the Shi'a. Even 'Ali, the paragon of Muslim chivalry, fell short of perfect chivalry on this occasion—at least in the Western sense of the word—though the advice he offered the Prophet was undoubtedly well meant, and in fact represented one of the inevitable human responses to a hopelessly tangled situation. Contradictions which are irreducible in human terms, however, may still be resolved by God in a single stroke; the hidden spiritual purpose of such contradictions may actually be to invoke such divine intervention, seeing that 'man's extremity is God's opportunity.' The following story of 'the affair of the necklace' recounts an instance of 'God's chivalry' that puts to shame all human attempts to achieve interpersonal justice, even that of the Prophet himself:

Once upon a march, when the caravan had stopped for rest, A'isha, the favorite wife of the Prophet Muhammad, peace and blessings be upon him, lost her necklace, and retraced her steps in order to find it. She did find it, but when she returned to where her camel had been resting, she saw that the entire caravan had departed. She decided to wait until they missed her and returned for her, and while waiting fell asleep. While she slept a straggler, Safwan, discovered her. He offered her his own camel's howdah, and led the camel on foot to the next stopping-place, where they caught up with the caravan.

In the following days, this incident led to rumors and speculations that A'isha and Safwan must have had a sexual encounter, and this nearly led to blows between the companions of the Prophet and those who had hatched the rumors. The Prophet defended A'isha in public (without letting her know, however), but this was not enough to silence the rumors; all, including Muhammad, were waiting for a revelation of the Qur'an to settle the question, but this was long delayed. (It should also be noted that, in line with the Arabic misogyny of the time, which was not far different from the misogyny of most other races in other places and times, it was A'isha, not Safwan, who was the main object of the slanderous rumors.)

The Prophet Muhammad, peace and blessings be upon him, was in a real quandary. This classic 'love triangle', though it only existed in the minds of the Muslims, was insoluble on its own level, as love triangles usually are. It created great stress in the lives of the Prophet, his wife, her rescuer, and the community at large, stress of the kind that could have torn that community apart.

The Prophet was in an unenviable position. If he accepted the slander as true he would be forced to punish his beloved wife without any real proof, but if he defended her openly he would appear as the cuckold, a man so dominated by an adulterous wife that, to his public shame, he was even forced to become her accomplice. If he ordered punishment of the slander-mongers on his own authority, he would appear to be self-servingly biased in favor of A'isha., but if he refrained, caving in to the slanderers, he would appear as weak before the people. Some of the Prophet's other wives defended A'isha to him, and the response of Ali ibn Abi Talib was: 'God has not restricted you, and there are many available women besides her. But question her maidservant and she will tell you the truth'. But of course no-one could replace A'isha in the eyes of the Prophet, because he loved her; he could take no solace from Ali's remark that, in effect, 'there are plenty of fish in the sea.' Following Ali's suggestion, A'isha's maid Burayrah was questioned on her impressions of A'isha's character, and she reported only good.

Finally the Prophet himself questioned her. Her answer was, 'I know that if I say I am guilty you will believe me, and if I say I am innocent you will not, but God knows I am guilty of nothing.' Then a new revelation of the Qur'an broke upon the Prophet: *Verily they who brought forth the lie are a party amongst you.... When ye took it upon your tongues, uttering with your mouths that whereof ye had no knowledge, ye counted it but a trifle. Yet in the sight of God it is enormous. Why said ye not when ye heard it: To speak of this is not for us. Glory be to Thee! This is a monstrous calumny. God biddeth you beware of ever repeating the like thereof, if ye are believers.* [Q. 24:15–17]

This is the archetype and the essence of Muslim chivalry — a chivalry capable of satisfying both the eastern and the western definitions of the word. Above and beyond all collective attitudes, prejudices and accommodations, this word of Allah establishes the pre-eminence of the *particular case* — as, precisely, does true romantic love. And note that the essence of such particularity, the cutting edge of it, is not an interested partiality with regard to the object of one's affections, but a rigorous and blade-like objectivity. Unless a man loves a woman as he loves truth, and *because* he loves truth, he is no spiritual romantic, at

least in the highest Western sense of the term as exemplified by
La Vita Nuova and *La Divina Commedia* by Dante Alighieri.

If Islam were truly to draw upon this depth of chivalry, from
God's direct word in the Holy Qur'an, it might even have the
power — with the help of the buried soul of Christendom awakened to new life—to restore a true spiritual chivalry (in a few
isolated instances, at least) to the Wasteland of the West. The
likelihood of such a development is seriously in doubt, however, given that even traditional Sufism, like certain strands of
ascetical Christianity, harbors attitudes that fall far short of the
heights of spiritual chivalry, especially in its Western rendition.
In *Masters of the Path: A History of the Masters of the Nimatullahi Sufi
Order*, Dr. Javad Nurbakhsh tells the story of Persian Sufi master
of the 1700s, Husayn 'Ali Shah, personally-chosen successor of
Nur 'Ali Shah, one of the most eminent masters in the history of
Persian Sufism. In his time and his culture, Husayn Ali Shah was
known for his spiritual poverty and detachment from the world.
He was also a victim of the common hatred of Sufis exhibited by
the exoteric mullas, one of whom ordered his execution—a fate
from which he was saved only by the direct intervention of the
Shah himself. In terms of the Persian society of his time, he was a
master of *adab* or spiritual courtesy. But in terms of traditional
Western courtesy—if a particular story told about him is true—
he fell far short, not of the all-too-common practice of the
West, regrettably, but certainly of the Western ideal. The story
is this:

> Husayn 'Ali Shah was a model in the realm of detachment
> (*tafrid*) and poverty (*faqr*). He never placed aside for himself
> any of the worldly wealth that was given to him by the der-
> vishes and admirers, but instead bestowed it all upon the
> needy, supporting himself and his wife with two carpet-
> making workshops which he inherited from his father.

> Husayn 'Ali Shah had an aged mother and a very bad-tem-
> pered wife who bickered and quarreled so with each other
> that some of his disciples begged him to divorce his wife
> and relieve himself of this burden. In response to them, he

said: 'If I divorce her, no one else will take care of her, and I'm afraid that she might not be able to endure the unmarried state and would fall into sin [presumably sexual promiscuity, if not prostitution]. Then I would be called to account. It's better that I continue living with her and tolerate her annoyance.' Thus, His Honor supported his wife and his mother, while he lived off yoghurt and bread in the college (*madrasah*) where he taught. For this reason, when guests came, his disciples would receive and entertain them. [p104]

In terms of the virtues admired and cultivated in the Islamic Persia of his time, this story is only to Husayn 'Ali Shah's credit. At the cost of personal suffering, he supported a wife he could legally have divorced, considering only her welfare, both material and spiritual. His practice was certainly much more conscientious than what has come to be fairly common practice in the contemporary West, where a wife of husband who 'doesn't work out' is often simply 'turned in for a better model.' Yet in terms of Western chivalry, which in a modified form became the code of the Western gentleman, he must be classed as an 'oaf'. An oaf is someone totally lacking in courtesy and sensitivity of feeling, who unthinkingly violates the sensibilities and hurts the feelings of those around him. An oaf is distinguished from a 'cad' by the fact that the cad violates the feelings of others cynically and deliberately, either out of pure maliciousness or for reasons of personal gain. A man who seduces and then abandons an innocent girl is a cad; a man who insults such a girl out of simple coarseness and social ignorance is an oaf. The 'chivalric' code of the western gentleman includes, but is certainly not limited to, the following rules: (1) One is not to speak of the shortcomings of one's wife, behind her back, with anyone whatsoever. This is the sin of 'backbiting', and represents a serious betrayal of the courtesy by which emotional and interpersonal values are preserved, as well as being a *de facto* violation of the marriage vow. (2) For any man to advise a gentleman to divorce his wife is not only a direct violation of all gentlemanly rules of conduct, but in certain places and times it would have required the gentleman so insulted to resort to arms defend his honor, and his wife's honor, at risk of his life. This ultimately derives from the Christian exaltation of marriage as a sacrament (akin to the Prophet Muhammad's teaching that 'marriage is half the religion'), which is the basis of the traditional Christian prohibition of divorce, based on Mark 9:10, 'Therefore what God hath joined together, let not man put asunder.' The *duel* which would sometimes have resulted may certainly be criticized as a barbaric institution in itself, as well as a violation of Christian values. But it did have the virtue of making clear to a human society vulnerable, as all societies are, to barbaric mores, the preeminence of the virtue of *honor*, as in the common chivalric motto, 'death before dishonor'. Of course honor itself is (or, as I suppose we must now say, *was*) ambiguous as a virtue, since it often meant no more than the choice to place one's reputation higher than any other value—higher than one's life, certainly, but also higher than one's humility, one's decency, and one's responsibility to protect those whom one loves. Honor has two faces: the fear of what would violate one's reputation in the eyes of society, and the fear of appearing dishonorable in one's own eyes, before the bar of one's conscience, which is the voice of God within one's heart. True chivalry gladly violates the first type of honor (cf. the episode 'The Knight of the Cart' from the *Launcelot* romance by Chretien de Troyes, recounted below), but trembles at any thought of violating the second. The man who says 'Whoever insults my wife insults *me*, and that I will not tolerate' is only worshipping his own ego. On the other hand, the man who says, 'If I let this man insult my wife without raising any protest, I am betraying her and causing her pain—and that I will not tolerate' is a true *chevalier*.

In the case of Husayn 'Ali Shah and his wife, anyone who understands western chivalry, and even certain aspects of common western sensibility, will immediately ask the following questions: How did the master's wife feel about his tendency to insult her in public, even to the point of implying that she would sink into promiscuity or prostitution without his continued influence and support? Could Husayn 'Ali Shah's willingness to publicly besmirch his wife's character have been at the origin of her tendency to bicker and quarrel? And though the quarrels are reported as being between the master's wife and his mother, could not Husayn 'Ali Shah possibly have had a hand in these difficulties as well, since he, like many western men who are overly attached to their mothers, is presented as taking his mother's part against his wife, assigning all the blame for the quarrels to his wife and none to his mother? Of course it is nearly impossible to answer these questions with any degree of certainty. Much time has passed, and the mores that operated effectively in Persian culture of 300 years ago are not applicable to the contemporary West. But it is certainly not out of place to ask them.

One might also ask, however, why the domestic squabbles of a famous Sufi and his wife and mother, centuries old, are relevant to us today. Why not let sleeping dogs lie? The answer is that my own spiritual Path, Islamic Sufism, has entered the West almost at the point of its death as a culture, and certainly after the point of its death as a spiritual culture. Many of the Sufis who have come West from eastern lands certainly know that they have walked into a barbaric world. What they do not and could not know is the original and living shape of the culture which lies in ruins all around them, and within whose corpse they have elected to take up residence; consequently they will be largely oblivious to forms of behavior that violate what was best in western culture, values that here and there still survive, though only in small pockets, or within the souls of isolated individuals who have been effectively silenced by the barbarism of contemporary society. This is why Seyyed Hossein Nasr proposes that Islamic universities endow departments of 'occidentalism' to match the 'orientalism' of the West—because Easterners, by and large, do not understand us, any better than we understand ourselves. And perhaps the worst thing that can happen to an eastern spirituality in the West is for it to feel an affinity for, and make common cause with, an aspect of degenerated western morality, because—by the craft of Eblis, apparently—this corruption of the collective western soul seems to show certain resemblances to something which, when the cultures of the East were healthy (for they, too, are dying), was the furthest thing from corruption. For example, the polygamy of Islam, based on the *sunnah* of the Prophet Muhammad, peace and blessings be upon him, was and is a viable social form, a seed-bed of virtue, tolerance, sensitivity and development of good character. In the West, where the highest ideal of relation between the sexes was a monogamy in which the element of romantic love was sobered, protected and deepened by the institution and sacrament of marriage, polygamy (but God knows best) can only represent the fall and corruption of what was deepest and finest in the western soul—a fall toward of the mores of the pimp. The *de facto* polygamy that shows some signs of developing in the West is concubinage, not marriage; it has no official social or religious sanction, and is often simply the result of the 'feminization of poverty' that follows upon the breakdown of the institution of western marriage, where women with reduced earning-power are forced to depend upon more affluent men, trading sexual favors for economic security. I hasten to say that I feel justified in applying this judgment on polygamy only to those born and raised in the West, not to immigrants from Islamic nations. Yet the cultural and psychic pollution of the dying West must affect them too, in ways that are too many and too subtle to detail. In these Latter Days of the human world, much must be branded and called to account for its sins; much, also, must be allowed to pass in silence, according to the common rule of western chivalry that 'discretion is the better part of valor.' In the words of the Prophet, 'No generation will come upon you that is not followed by a worse', and: 'In this time, those who fail to fulfill only a tenth of the law will inherit the Fire; while in the latter days, those who fulfill only a tenth of the law will inherit the Garden.'

As Frithjof Schuon has pointed out, all traditional religions have a streak of misogyny in them. The writer of the Book of Job, as well as those Islamic sages who composed the humorous and symbolic Nasruddin stories, could represent Job's or Nasruddin's wife, unblushingly, as symbols of the lower self. And as we have already seen, the unashamed and truly *foul* misogyny of many traditional Christian monks (and Buddhist monks as well) is equally notorious. But there were always other spiritual tendencies in the West that countered this spiritual misogyny, notably the western tradition of spiritualized romantic love, perhaps best represented by the troubadour poet Arnaut Daniel, by the greatest of the Arthurian romancers, Wolfram Von Eschenbach, and certainly by the greatest of all Christian poets, Dante Aligheri, in his figure of Beatrice. And this western romantic tradition, as is well known, owed a great deal to the Arabo-Persian poetic tradition, a tradition with Sufi affiliations, that entered Western Europe through the crusades, through the culturally Islamicized imperial court of Sicily, and through Muslim Spain. As I already pointed out, one of the tributaries to this tradition was the school of the *udri* poets of 11th century Islam, who deferred to and idealized their chosen Ladies in terms nearly identical to the western troubadours, and who considered romantic love— whether chaste or consummated—as one of the most powerful ways of developing and refining the human character. The same system of sentiments was echoed by the Andalusian writer Ibn Hazm in his book *The Dove's Neck-ring*, which is thought to be the direct ancestor of *The Art of Loving Honestly* by Andreas Capellanus, the central prose textbook of the western romantic tradition, commissioned by Eleanor of Aquitaine herself. Capellanus, Dante, Boccaccio, Guido Cavalcanti, the painter Pedro de Pisa, Petrarch, Cardinal Francesco Barberino, Dino Compagni, and Brunetto Latini are thought by some scholars to have been members of the *Fedeli d'Amore* or *Fede Santa*, a secret initiatory order which used both the allegory and the actual practice of romantic love as a spiritual method. As we have seen above, such great figures in Sufism as Ruzbehan Baqli have been classed by some as among 'the Fedeli d'Amore of Islam,' while affinities and possible ties have been discerned between the western Fedeli d'Amore and both to the Knights Templars, the flower of western chivalry, who respected Islam even while fighting against it in the Crusades, and the Sufi order known as the Shadiliyya.

Most of this, however, is forgotten, to be recalled only by scholarly specialists; in terms of western culture, romantic love has lost its force, except as something to be attacked, parodied, slandered and inverted. (I was born in 1948; it took its last breath in my lifetime.) And when a latter-day Sufism meets a slandered and corrupted tradition of western romance, whatever may have been their close ties and shared outlook in the distant past, a degree of irony is reached that can only be produced by a fall from an exalted cultural and spiritual station into a bubbling morass where cross-cultural misunderstanding and inter-cultural degeneration meet and mingle. And one of the most dire possibilities in such a cultural wasteland would be for the characteristic misogyny of Islam—which, for all its limitations and undeniable abuses, most of which grew up after the time of the Prophet and were often opposed to his *sunnah*, once had a real cultural place—to meet and interbreed with the new misogyny of the West that has sprung from the decay of one of our deepest spiritual traditions, that of romantic love. Is this were to happen, any hope of resurrecting the Fedeli d'Amore (in its generic not its initiatory sense, I hasten to add), of restoring and refining the character and spirituality of the West, whose wholesale corruption produced Abu Ghraib, and of resurrecting any semblance of Western chivalry, would be forlorn indeed. Yet God Himself does not degenerate, only our faith in Him: *all is perishing except His Face.* The remembrance of God retains the power, God willing, to awaken the generations of the dead within the human soul, bring them to life, and turn them toward that living Face.

IV. An Example of Divinely Inspired Courtesy from the Noble Qur'an, and the Degeneration of This Virtue

The history of Sufism contains many glowing examples of heroic self-effacement in the sphere of interpersonal relations. But as we have already seen in the case of *surah* 24, 'an-Nur', the Noble Qur'an represents a higher standard of chivalry than anything in Sufi literature, precisely because the Qur'an is both the direct Word of God, and the ultimate origin of any Sufism worthy of the name. This higher chivalry appears once again in the *surah* 80, 'He Frowned'; the occasion for the revelation of this *surah* was the following:

Once when Muhammad was giving audience, a blind man, Ibn Maktoom, tried to get his attention in a way that annoyed him; the Prophet frowned and turned away. In response to this, he received the *surah* 'He Frowned', which corrected Muhammad's behavior. There is something almost sublime in the fact that a slight, subtle, momentary lapse in *adab* (courtesy) on the Prophet's part was allowed by God, or even in a way willed by Him, in order to establish that Muhammad was *'abd* (God's slave) as well as *khalifa* (God's appointed representative), and also to demonstrate Muhammad's perfect openness to reproof; in this he is truly an example for Muslims. (This *surah*, in reproving Muhammad, also compensates in a way for the *surah* 24, which— to those harboring secret doubts as to whether the Qur'an is actually the Revealed Word of God—might otherwise have seemed to be self-serving.) We are not perfect; only Allah is perfect. But we may still perfectly respond to God's reproof, as the Prophet demonstrated on this occasion. For the Qur'an to reprove Hind or Abu Lahab, archetypal enemies of Islam, is not unexpected; for it to reprove its own chosen revelatory instrument is tremendous. A tiny imperfection that most of us would not even notice in ourselves became the occasion for the revelation of a portion of God's Eternal Word. Allah appears to be emphasizing here that the little, day-to-day lapses in courtesy that all of us fall into and think of as not even worthy of notice are really of immense import. Under the screen of the collective social trance, they break people's hearts, and then condemn them to suffer in silence—if for no other reason than that it would seem excessive, even to the offended ones, to raise an objection about a mere look, even if it cut to the heart. (Ibn Maktoom could not see the Prophet's frown, but the elders of the Quraysh did, and Ibn Maktoom might have heard some murmur from them, or felt a chill come over the room.) Moses (peace and blessings be upon him) was sent to denounce heartless and moribund social hierarchies; Jesus (peace and blessings be upon him), to preach against loveless pride of religion; and Muhammad (peace and blessings be upon him), via the Qur'an and his *sunnah*, partly to sweep away social *coarseness*. He brought a general refinement of manners to a very coarse and unfeeling society—one where female infanticide was common, for example—and even instituted things like oral hygiene. And not the least of the reforms he brought was a strong reminder that one crucial element in the kind of sensitivity of feeling we used to call 'gentlemanly' or 'civilized' in the West is the ability to immediately sense when offense has been given, and be willing to soothe wounded feelings quickly, sincerely and without hesitation. We underestimate the degree of self-effacement this often requires. To people of certain character types, in certain social situations, to openly admit that one has unthinkingly given offense is like *dying*; the individual in question would rather commit murder than apologize, since to do so would destroy his or her entire sense of self-worth, which (whether he realizes this or not) has become completely identified with social vanity, if not murderous aggression. As our society continues its descent into sub-human barbarism, the ability to apologize without an excruciating loss of face is fast disappearing. Some people—I'm thinking particularly of gang mores here, which seem to be spreading, slowly but surely, throughout our society—would literally rather be shot than humble themselves to apologize.

Gang mores entered mainstream western society through the counterculture of the 60's and 70's. I know of one sector of that counterculture from personal experience—the San Francisco poetry scene of the 1970's—where it was believed that to insult a man's wife in his presence was a good way of *currying favor* with him, on the theory of 'we guys need to stick together against the bitches.' These mores are, precisely, the mores of the pimp, as detailed in Claude Brown's autobiography of his life of crime in New York City's Harlem in the 50's and 60's, *Manchild in the Promised Land*. The pimp must hold power over his women at all cost. He must treat them well only to control them; he must never fall in love with them, and never beg them for sexual favors. And like many of the folkways of the 'underclass,' the mores of the black pimp of post-WWII Harlem have spread far and wide through western society in the past few decades.

V: Chivalry and Romance

But let us return to the question of the relationship between chivalry and romance.

In Medieval European society, the legal status of women as chattels of their men was compensated for by the exaltation of the Lady, by both the troubadours and Arthurian romancers—an exaltation that reached its pinnacle in Dante's figure of Beatrice in the *Divine Comedy*, who functions there as a type of Holy Wisdom, and thus necessarily, in Christian terms, as a reflection of the Virgin Mary. In a medieval context the near adoration of the Lady undoubtedly had a *malamati* quality, at least to begin with; in a society where official Christianity tended to denigrate women—all veneration of the Virgin apart—a exaltation of womanhood might cause a man to be seen as a weakling, a degenerate, or both; one of the conventions discernible in the Arthurian romances, partly hidden by the mores of a later time and place (specifically, those of the courts of southern France beginning in the 11th century where such exaltation was more socially acceptable), was that a man's love for his Lady, like Majnun's love for Layla, might open him to madness (if not adultery), and thus to social disgrace. Nonetheless, down to the early 20th century, the exaltation of womanhood, at least on some level, was an integral part of social honor and gentlemanly conduct—though hard-headed worldly cynics might always have looked at a man who wanted to 'tell the world' of his love for his Lady as a kind of impractical fool. Ever since Cervantes' *Don Quixote* (A.D. 1605), chivalry and romance were in danger of being viewed as 'quixotic'; still, until perhaps the end of the 1950's, they still functioned, along with the more Christian virtues of faith, hope, charity, prudence, justice, fortitude, and temperance, as a pillar of 'polite' society in the western world.

One of the problems encountered by any man who wants to

chivalrously defend his beloved against insult or social obloquy is that it will seem to be self-serving. For me to defend the poor, the suffering and the voiceless will be considered admirable, but since my wife or fiancée is seen by profane society as nothing but as extension of my ego, for me to 'chivalrously' defend her is treated as nothing but a vain and egotistical attempt to defend myself. And so, unless I am willing to be considered both a self-serving hypocrite and a fool, I had better not defend my wife; the socially wiser course will be for me to say, 'baby, you're on your own,' which is essentially to allow society to put us into competition against each other for approval and acclaim, not to mention economic success. (The 65% divorce rate in the United States is sufficient evidence of the real effect of such degenerate social mores, which amount to little more than a curse laid upon love and faithfulness between a man and a woman.) And, in one of the greatest social ironies of our time, the *feminists* have routinely supported such mores, and have had a large hand in creating them. Feminism is nothing but simple justice when it calls for equal work for equal pay, paid maternity leave etc. But when it turns against marriage, against romance, against love and faith and *justice* between the sexes, then it becomes one more element—well-disguised but not perfectly so—in the social oppression of women, particularly women of the lower classes. To the degree that feminism in the West is an expression of the ambitions of women of the professional class, to whom marriage is often secondary, the attack on marriage as a 'patriarchal' institution cleverly disguises an attack on those declassé women to whom marriage is still central, or to whom it would be central if it were not for that very attack. The following story illustrates this dynamic:

In a recent women's golf tournament, the winner of the million-dollar first prize was a young Latina. The oversized check was presented to her by a feminist, who declared that 'this victory is a victory for all women.' It was not a victory for those women who *lost* the tournament, however; and the feminist's attempt to portray the winner as somehow a victor in the war between the sexes was specifically designed to hide the fact that, if it was a victory for anyone beside the winner herself, it was a victory for the Latinos, the vast U.S. underclass, since the girl who won the tournament had dedicated most of prize money to the construction of a school in her home town in Mexico.

Women today are taught to see any man's chivalrous attempt to defend them from attack as 'condescending', and thus as an attack in itself. And to the degree that women repel any attempt on a man's part to defend them, they are in effect working to turn men from vigorous defenders into powerless spectators, and ultimately into attackers themselves, whether through passive aggression or active violence. And inseparable from a women's rejection of a man's innate desire—if he is a man of honor—to defend her is her unstated belief that *she is not worth defending*. To the degree that this society requires every man and woman to be ruthlessly ambitious, it requires them to be 'hustlers'—in other words, prostitutes. The upper middle class woman will consider the sort of ambition that leads her to sacrifice her husband and even her children if they get in her way as an admirable trait, and look down upon the lower class women who must depend economically upon men as 'cheap', and the families or liaisons they find themselves in as 'dysfunctional'. Yet to the degree that both classes reject husband and children (I am *not* referring here to women who remain single) in order to maintain their livelihoods, thus sacrificing the good of future generations, both may be considered prostitutes in effect—not necessarily because they have chosen this role, but because society has imposed it upon them, given that it needs to produce more and more prostitutes every day in order to function according to the standards upon which it is presently based. And when a man attempts to defend a woman who considers herself to be of no intrinsic worth outside her economic or social achievements, he in effect confronts her with the truth that she *feels* like a prostitute, or simply like a loser; no wonder she reacts violently against such defense. (I should add here that there are plenty of men of the lower classes who, like the pampered momma's-boys of the rich, depend upon women, and seem to pride themselves on the so-called 'power' they have, through charm and threat, to make women support them.) It is true that some forms of male defense of women *are* condescending, particularly when they function as screens for subtle manipulation; a society that must set all its members at war with each other, and must do everything it can to destroy the family since it recognizes in 'family values' a center of social power not yet entirely under the control of the dominant political and economic forces, will do its best to turn even courteous and self-sacrificing defense of the defenseless into insult, manipulation and oppression. But it is clear from a survey of the pertinent western literature that chivalry in its original form—which, though it may have been no more than an ideal, was still the ideal of real men— had nothing to do with condescension or manipulation. It was a way of saluting a woman's intrinsic worth, the source of her socially-sanctioned power to call forth honorable and chivalrous and self-sacrificing defense on the part of men, a mode of feminine power universally recognized as inseparable from a woman's honor.

A good illustration of this chivalric ideal appears in the *Launcelot* romance, in the episode known as 'The Knight of the Cart'. Queen Guinevere has been kidnapped by an evil knight, and the knights of Arthur's round table fan out in search of her. On his way Sir Launcelot encounters a dwarf driving a cart, and it is explained to the reader that in those days such carts represented a profound social shame; any man of good reputation who mounted one was eternally disgraced. The dwarf calls out to Sir Launcelot: 'Get into my cart and I'll tell you where the Queen is.' Launcelot hesitates for a split second, then gets in. After many adventures and battles, which include crossing a moat on a bridge consisting of a keen sword-blade, which cuts deeply into the knight's hands and feet, he finally rescues the Queen—and the first thing she says is: 'You *hesitated* before getting into the cart! You have covered yourself with shame!' And Launcelot humbly submits. The split second in which he placed his reputation above the Queen's welfare has seriously compromised his honor, and not even all his subsequent sufferings and exploits, even his successful rescue of her, have paid the debt incurred in that moment. The Queen here (besides apparently being omniscient) is obviously the carrier of a transpersonal value of the highest spiritual import. It is clear, however, that as a society we can no longer see women in this way, even in mythological terms. We can no longer grant them this kind of essentially feminine power, a power based on the sense of their intrinsic value, whether or not they may have fully actualized that value in their personal lives. If they are not intellectual or physical or sexual or magical Amazons, the equivalent of Xena Warrior Princess or Hillary Clinton, if they are not as skillful as men, or more so, in their ability to wield essentially masculine powers, then we can no longer recognize their spiritual *numinosity*; all we know how to do is treat them as if they were nothing but unsuccessful men.

As the collective sense of the reality of God and the metaphysical order continues to erode in the West, so does the sense of a person's intrinsic worth, a worth based not on what a person does or achieves, but what a person *is*. When Christianity was culturally strong, it was possible to see a human being in terms of the *imago dei*, as 'made in the image and likeness of God,' rather than simply as a product of genetic inheritance and social conditioning; the intrinsic worth of someone was recognized as a *transpersonal* reality, not merely a personalistic one. But as the sense of 'it is not I who live but Christ lives in me' faded from our culture, it was inevitable that persons would be seen as *egos* alone, with nothing transcendent or spiritual whatsoever underlying those egos. And someone who is defined solely in egoistic terms can have no eternal or intrinsic worth, only a more-or-less well developed ability to succeed in material and psychological terms, to get ahead in the world, to command other people's attention, admiration, or fear. Under this kind of false, shrunken, materialistic definition of the human being, those who cannot easily do these things are not simply unsuccessful; they are literally worthless. Women don't want to be 'put on pedestals' any longer in the West because they don't feel they can live up to such adulation—which, insofar as they are defined as egos alone, they obviously can't. And to be praised for something one knows one cannot live up to is, ultimately, to feel degraded. The truth is, there is nothing more difficult and burdensome for a woman than to be seen as the bearer of a transpersonal, spiritual value that she, by her own efforts, could never merit. In chivalric terms, for a woman to submit to being defended by a man is to suffer every bit as much as her defender must suffer, though in the opposite way. The chivalrous man must endure not only the outer blows of the enemy, social or military, but also the inner blows of his conscience, his 'accusing self', his sense of his own unworthiness to adequately defend the woman he has undertaken to protect. Likewise the woman who submits to this protection must suffer the blows of her own accusing self, her sense that she is in no way worthy of the sacrifices being made on her behalf. Chivalry calls us to be better than ourselves, and in so doing humbles us before our own ideals.

But these ideals are not simply wishes or fantasies; they are objective realities that carry the potential of being concretely realized. The woman who allows herself to be the object of chivalrous defense must in some sense actually incarnate the values that make her worthy of such defense, just as the man who undertakes to defend her must actually be worthy of that calling. Both must 'meet the mark', and the mark they must meet is the inherent dignity of the human state. This human dignity is called, in Muslim terms, *al-fitrah*, the original human nature; in Christian terms that soul is based on the *imago dei*, the image of God within the human soul, without which that soul could not properly be called human. As the *hadith* says, 'Heaven and earth cannot contain Me, but the heart of my willing slave can contain Me.' The image of the noble lady the chivalrous man swears to defend is not simply a projection of his own unconscious femininity upon the object of his attention—an 'anima-projection' as the Jungians would say—but a true recognition of an objective Reality that lies within her. As Ibn al-'Arabi put it, in his chapter 'The Wisdom of Singularity [i.e. *particularity*, uniqueness] in the Word of Muhammad' from the *Fusus al-Hikam*:

the Apostle [Muhammad] loved women by reason of perfect contemplation of Reality in them. Contemplation of

Reality without formal support is not possible, since God, in his Essence, is far beyond all need of the Cosmos. Since, therefore, some form of support is necessary, the best and most perfect kind is the contemplation of God in women.

Likewise Jalaluddin Rumi says, in the *Mathnawi*, 1/2531–35: 'she [woman] is a ray of God, she is not that [earthly] beloved: she is creative, you must say she is not created.'

VI: The Essence of Chivalry

Metaphysical principles are eternal. Virtues, the human reflection of such principles, are relatively so, being co-extensive with the human race. Mores, however, are mutable. For example, the virtue of courage, though it will always be required when we struggle for livelihood, go into combat or face inevitable pain or death, will change in its application—though not in its essence—as the form of its enemy changes: on the psycho-social level, while we may always fear social disapproval (until we finally break with the Darkness of This World), the forms this disapproval takes, and the specific actions or qualities of character that invoke it, will change over time. In order to defend the weak and oppressed in psycho-social rather than strictly military terms, in order to combat oppressive and largely unconscious social mores (given that we tend to become unconscious of anything we take for granted), we need to know the specific forms social oppression and egotism take in particular places and times. Groups have egos as well as individuals; the ego of a given society in a given historical period will exalt some human traits and denigrate others in a different way than another society or historical period would do. Books like *The Way of Sufi Chivalry* contain inspiring stories of heroic chivalry and courtesy in the social and interpersonal realms, some of which will be immediately applicable in any place or time. But as we have already seen, certain other stories in books like that, or certain nuances in stories that for the most part still remain relevant, will not easily divulge their full meaning and application in

places and times where the *enemy*, the collective egotism of society and its reflection within the individual, takes a different
form. We need to know exactly where the group ego is situated
and how its reverberations play out within the individual
psyche; if we do not, certain stories of chivalry from ages past
may end by be taken as models for various forms of automatic
behavior that *symbolize* chivalry for us, but do not in fact represent it. Simply acting in an external way like Persian Sufis of 700
years ago, for example, or like European knights and ladies of
the 12ᵗʰ Century, is largely a waste of effort.

Nonetheless chivalry remains intimately related to war, which
is why the traditional chivalric literature of the West has to do
with knights, with armed combatants. This war is not necessarily
fought with swords or guns, but war it is, and nothing else. It is war
against the collective egotism of a given society, or social class, or
group. Every human collectivity has its own ego, its own *nafs al-
ammara*, as we saw above in the story of the 'affair of the necklace',
where the collective attitudes of the Muslims were at odds with
the *particular case* of A'isha, who was slandered, yet blameless.
Every group 'taxes' the individual egos of its members to finance
its own collective ego, which in turn 'charters' the individual egos
of its members, 'validating' them if they obey it and 'cursing' them
if, consciously or unconsciously, they violate its sometimes
explicit but often unwritten laws. It was in recognition of this
truth that William Blake said 'corporeal friends are spiritual
enemies,' and 'a man's worst enemies are of his own house and
family.' Only after great spiritual struggle can an individual
become fully aware of his own *nafs al-ammara*—and for a group,
especially a large group, to become aware of its collective *nafs* may
not be possible until the Day of Judgment. Yet the spiritual
chevalier, the *javanmard*, must not only be aware of his own
tendencies to egotism, but also of the character and agendas of
the group-ego he is called by God to confront in chivalric combat.
The *javanmard* is sworn to defend the helpless and the oppressed,
and there is virtually no social oppression that does not involve
the tyranny of some form of collective egotism over an oppressed
and helpless individual. I say 'individual', not 'individuals,' because

chivalry always involves the defense of the *particular case* (as with A'isha) against the collective norm. Some collective norms, such as the *shari'ah*, are instituted by God; others, like the Confucian ideal or the liberal democratic ideals of the West, are built by enlightened men. In any viable human culture, certain collective norms of behavior must exist; to violate such norms necessarily leads to social chaos, and is therefore justly classed as criminal. But when the ego of a group or society or religion usurps and disguises itself beneath the legitimate norms on which these collectives are built, a condition of oppression exists. And to alleviate this oppression, chivalrous action is called for. Such action must be based on a subtler and more penetrating insight into situations than anything collective norms, even at their best, can provide. Such insight is necessary in order to discern the exact shape the ego of the collective has taken in a given oppressive situation, and the specific kind of intervention necessary to counter it. Good intentions and general rules of behavior are not enough; they themselves may in fact be part of the oppressive system that needs to be overturned, given that unconsciousness can transform the letter of a legitimate rule into a subversion and violation of the spirit of that very rule.

Chivalry is armed courtesy. Its sword is invisible, but no less sharp for all that—far sharper, in fact, than the dull, sleepy swords of habitual assumptions and social stereotypes. And, like *dhu l'fiqar* ('double-pointed,' the sword of Imam Ali), it cuts two ways: whenever the *javanmard* sees a social evil, he takes this as a sign that an analogous evil exists in himself. Not in himself alone, certainly; there is no use or real intelligence in employing one's own moral self-examination to deny the reality of evil in the outer world. To do so is a subtle way of shirking one's responsibility to succor the oppressed, to extend help when help is needed. We are not God; our individual psyche is not the whole world; to act as if it were is to deny the reality of people other than ourselves, and there is nothing more unchivalrous than this. It's simply that we tend to encounter in the outer world, as real, objective evils affecting real people, the very evils we also harbor within our own souls. Prophets and saints, of course, are far beyond this dynamic; the Prophet Muhammad, peace and blessings be upon him, was able to go into chivalrous combat against the degenerate mores of the Pagan Arabs of his time not because he himself was infected by them, but because, by God's grace, he had already been purified of them.

Chivalry, then—including romantic chivalry—can be defined as the set of spiritual duties that is laid upon us as we approach the border between the lesser *jihad* against degenerate social mores, and the greater *jihad* against the corruption of the *nafs al-ammara*, the 'self commanding to evil'. Whoever shirks the outer battle against the Rulers of the Darkness of This World, to the degree that God confronts him or her with it directly, is no *jav-anmard*, but whoever fails to fight this battle in service to and as a necessary part of the 'war against the soul' is no *darvish*.

In many medieval romances, both Muslim and Christian, the beloved can only be won after overcoming dangerous trials, which often include slaying a monster or a dragon or an evil knight. It's as if a kind of adulterous love-triangle exists between a Princess, a Dragon who keeps her captive, and a Hero who rescues her. One way we can look at stories like this is as a picture of what is going on in our own inner world. From this point of view, the Hero is our will and rational intelligence in service to our conscience or 'accusing self', trying their best to follow what seems to be true and worthy, fighting against everything low and false, and sometimes going mad in the process. (Madness symbolizes the intuition of a Reality higher than conscious will and rational intelligence.) The Dragon is our mass of unredeemed passions, our unconscious ego, the 'commanding self' which holds our soul, the Princess, in bondage. (In Nizami's romance of *Layla and Majnun*, the 'dragon' appears, at one point, as Layla's family, who want to keep the lovers separated because they see Majnun's love-madness as socially shameful and dishonorable.) And the Princess, rescued from the commanding self, is the 'self-at-peace'—our power to submit, in 'unadulterated' purity, to the Will of God. Thus the suffering and that romantic love requires, and the chivalrous battle that is inseparable from it, is not ultimately of the body, or of this or that outer enemy, but of the ego itself. In the armed contest to win the true Beloved, the *nafs al-ammara* is the only rival; it is precisely at the point where this truth is realized that the lesser *jihad* is transformed into the greater. A man's ego, his commanding self, is the adversary of both his human beloved and his own spiritual Heart—even (or especially!) when it appears as *the ego of chivalry itself.*

In the *Parzival* romance of Wolfram von Eschenbach, the chivalrous ego, the pride of love and war, is symbolized by King Anfortas, whose war-cry is '*Amor!*' As punishment for this *hubris*, he is wounded in the testicles during a joust; his wound never kills him, but it never heals. And due to it (though this particular episode appears not in Wolfram but in the *Perlesvaus* romance) his kingdom becomes a wasteland. Almost the whole action of the romance, all the quests, the trysts, and the passages-at-arms of the heroes Parzival and Gawain, is for the ultimate purpose of healing the wounded king. Thus *Parzival* is the story of the struggle to overcome the pride of love and war through love and war themselves. Because nothing exalts us, and nothing humbles us, like these two arts. Without the glory of war no-one would find the courage fight even the most necessary battles; without the glamour of love, no-one would ever risk hurling himself into the current of life, and living with a whole heart. But inevitable death and loss lie in wait for both the lover and the warrior; without these terribly humbling experiences, their two paths could never reach perfection. And the most humbling possible experience, for a chivalrous man, is the realization that his will to defend a beloved woman—in whose person he also defends the whole realm of feeling-values, which is also an aspect of his own higher self—is, at a certain point, the very enemy she needs to be defended against. God Alone is her true Defender; for a man to egotistically impose his chivalry upon a woman, no matter how idealistically he does it, is to come between her and God, and so become her oppressor—and his own as well. The most chivalrous possible act, then, is to commend one's Lady to God, and rest in God oneself; this is the most chaste and the most loving of all possible unions. If it is chivalry to sacrifice one's life for the sake of one's beloved, then this is that very death.

The Knights Templars
and the Holy Grail

Since speculations on the supposed esoteric knowledge and function of the Knights Templars, the history and meaning of the Holy Grail, and the relation of the Grail to the Templars routinely turn up in scholarship (esoteric or otherwise) relating to the chivalric and romantic traditions, it is time now to consider a bit of lore on these subjects.

René Guénon identifies the Templars as the guardians of the Primordial Tradition in the Christian Middle Ages. The Primordial Tradition is the original spiritual revelation of God to Man, and *as* Man, insofar as we are made 'in the image and likeness of God'. This is why the Jews and Muslims name Adam as the first prophet. Tradition knows the cycle of manifestation as a progressive departure from Source; and so the time had to come when the Primordial Tradition could no longer be known in undiluted form. This is the point pictured in the legend of the fall of the Tower of Babel, which represents the Promethean attempt of titanic, fallen humanity to take heaven by storm, but only after the primordial connection to Source had already been broken. The Tower, like any ziggurat, is itself a symbol of the *axis mundi*, the cosmic prolongation of, and spiritual Way back to, that Source. Every sacred mountain, sacred tree, etc., as well as the erect stature of the human form itself (epitomized in the 'upright' man, the *tzaddik*), is a reflection of the *axis mundi*. Muhammad (peace and blessings be upon him) was transported in his Night Journey from Mecca to Jerusalem—to the Temple Mount—from which he ascended along the *axis mundi* to the higher worlds. So Jerusalem is related to the *axis mundi* in an Islamic context, just as it is (via the *Divine Comedy*, for example) in a Christian one.

According to Guénon, the Templars knew and held to the Polar Source of all the revealed religions, particularly the Abrahamic ones, which explains their occupation of the Temple Mount, sacred to all three Abrahamic religions, after the First Crusade. But since religions cannot be mixed in the world of form without polluting them and invoking demonic forces, their lore was *arcane,* to be kept hidden in an *ark,* such as the First Temple once held.

In *Symbols of Sacred Science,* Guénon has much to say about the symbolism of the *cornerstone,* traditionally identified with Jesus, which in the Gospels is 'the headstone of the corner' that the builders rejected—just as the Jews, the builders of the Temple, rejected Christ. (He is careful, however, to identify the 'headstone of the corner' not with the cornerstone of a foundation but with the capstone of an arch.) Guénon connects it with the philosophers' stone, with the Kaaba and its Black Stone, with the Jerusalem Temple and thus, by extension, with the Templars. Undoubtedly it also has affinities with the Rock on the Temple Mount, above which the Dome of the Rock, *al-Aqsa Masjid,* is built—the Rock upon which, according to legend, Abraham was poised to sacrifice his son, until God stayed his hand. (In the most Templar-influenced of the Arthurian romances, the *Parzival* of Wolfram Von Eschenbach, the Holy Grail is not a cup but a stone.) 'Headstone of the corner' in Latin is *caput anguli,* the 'head of the angle'; in Arabic this phrase is rendered as *rukn al-arkan* ('angle of angles'), which can also be translated as 'summit'. The five *arkan* (angles) in certain strands of Islamic esoterism are the major principles or *arcana* of the cosmos, and are related to the five elements; the 'summit' angle corresponds to aether, the quintessence.

If the four elements are angles, crowned with a fifth 'summit' angle, we have the image of a pyramid, and thus are square within Masonic lore. (The Masons picked up certain Templar influences after the suppression of the Order at the beginning of the fourteenth century.) Guénon saw Freemasonry as a valid, though largely degenerate, initiatic organization, perhaps originally a Sufi order. He believed that Masonic symbolism was

metaphysically accurate, but no-one can deny that the Masons
have often lent themselves to beliefs and activities which were
both spiritually and politically subversive. The Masonic myth of
human *edification*—as in our word 'edifice'—of the building of
the Temple of Man, may have been true and effective in a context which recognizes God's grace as the primary agent, but outside such a context it becomes Promethean, making the Tower
of Babel a more appropriate symbol than the First Temple at
Jerusalem of later Masonry, one more related to Antichrist than
to Christ Jesus. In the words of Psalm 27, 'Except the Lord build
the house, they labor in vain who build it.'

On pages 43–44 of *Insights into Christian Esoterism*, Guénon, following Luigi Valli, and within the general context of the Templars, mentions the peregrinations of initiates as forming a
hidden aspect of pilgrimage. Were such esoteric pilgrims to be
found among the Templars? Was the founding of the Order of
the Temple, as an armed response to the threat posed to the pilgrimage routes by the Muslim conquests, partly inspired by
such pilgrims? Guénon identifies the Templars as among the
'Guardians of the Holy Land' of the Primordial and Unitary Tradition, in relation to the assertion of the figure of Melchizedek
in the *Decamerone* of Boccaccio—named as among the Fedeli
d'Amore, who in turn have sometimes been describes as a kind
of 'third order' of the Templars—that no one knows whether
Judaism, Christianity or Islam is the true religion.

Could the Templars have occupied the Temple Mount in
Jerusalem partly to prevent the other crusaders from destroying
the Dome of the Rock, thus combining the exoteric role of
Christian holy warriors against Islam with the more esoteric
function of preserving Jerusalem as a point-of-origin for the
unitary Tradition by preventing it from being *monopolized* by
Islam? The report of Usama ibn Munqidh, Emir of Shaizar, that
the Templars used to put an oratory attached to the Dome of
the Rock at his disposal so that he could pray, and that they
defended his right to do so against Frankish 'newcomers' (cf.
Edward Burman, *The Templars, Knights of God*, 1986, Destiny
Books, p76) can be explained by the fact that it would have been

equally in line with this (conjectural) agenda for the Templars to prevent the sanctuary from being monopolized by the *Christians*. Nothing would have more effectively cloaked this purpose than the Templar presence as part of the Christian army of occupation! It might also explain their recklessly brave but often strategically unsound war-making: better suffer high casualties than ever be suspected of an 'esoteric' collaboration with the enemy. (Making obeisance to Saladin was one of the charges brought against them at their trial—a charge that would have seemed patently absurd unless rumors to that effect had already become associated with the Order over a period of time.)

The association of the Templars with the Holy Grail, which we find in Wolfram von Eschenbach's *Parzival* romance (and elsewhere), also identifies them as guardians of the Primordial Tradition, because the Grail is, among other things, an emblem of the Virgin Mary, the vessel that held the body and blood of Christ when He lay in her womb—and Mary was called by the great Sufi Ruzbehan Baqli 'the Mother of all the Prophets', i.e., all the prophets of the Abrahamic tradition. The Virgin is further associated with the Templars by the fact that St. Bernard, who composed the rule of the Order, called the Virgin Mary his 'Lady' in the style of Courtly Love; the epithet 'Our Lady' may even have originated with him.

According to legend, the Grail received either the sacramental blood of Christ at the Last Supper, or His fleshly blood at the Crucifixion. That blood was spilled from the heart of Christ by the spear of Longinus. When Jesus was first presented in the Temple, the Prophet Simeon called Him 'Thy [God's] salvation, which Thou hast prepared before the face of all the people', and said to the Virgin, 'Behold, this child is set for the fall and rising again of many in Israel, and a sign which shall be spoken against (yea, a sword shall pierce through thy own soul also), that the thoughts of many hearts may be revealed' [Luke 2:30-31;34-35]. According to Frithjof Schuon in *Dimensions of Islam*, the chapter 'The Wisdom of Sayyidatna Maryam', 'Maryam [the name of the Virgin Mary in Arabic] belongs to Judaism by her personality in fact [i.e., the fact that she was a Jew], to Christianity by her special

function, and to Islam by her supereminence in the whole Abrahamic cosmos.' The Qur'an itself says of Mary: . . . *the angels said: O
Mary! Lo! Allah hath chosen thee and made three pure, and hath preferred
thee above all the women of creation.* Mary is closely associated with
the Jerusalem Temple in the Gospels, and according to Eastern
Orthodox tradition was a 'maiden' dedicated to Temple service;
her initiation into this function is celebrated in the Orthodox
calendar by the feast of the Entrance into the Temple.

The story is as follows: The parents of the Virgin, Joachim and
Anna, when praying for God to overcome their barrenness,
vowed that if a child was born it would be dedicated to the service of God. Thus when the Virgin Mary was three years old, her
parents resolved to fulfill their vow. They gathered relatives and
acquaintances, clothed Mary in bright garments, and led her to
the Jerusalem Temple, singing sacred hymns and carrying lit
candles in their hands. There the Virgin was met by the High
Priest. Leading up into the Temple were fifteen high steps, and
the child Mary was not strong enough to climb these steps on
her own. But as soon as she was put on the first step God
strengthened her, and she quickly climbed the remaining steps
to the top. Later, following a Divine inspiration, the High Priest
led the Virgin into the Holy of Holies, the most sacred place in
the Temple into which he himself was normally allowed to
enter only once a year on behalf of the people, after first making
sacrifices for them and for himself. All present were astonished
at this extraordinary event.

According to Eastern Orthodox tradition, the Virgin Mary
spent a period of time in Jerusalem, during which she was edu-
cated in the community of pious virgins, diligently read the
Holy Scriptures, and occupied herself with handiworks, and
perpetual prayer. Mary's Entrance into the Temple is also echoed in the Noble Qur'an, in the surah *Mary*, verse 16: *And make
mention of Mary in the Scripture, when she had withdrawn from her people into a chamber looking East*—which was the direction the High
Priest faced in the Jerusalem Temple on Yom Kippur, the Day of
Atonement.

Glastonbury Abbey, possibly the earliest Christian site in Britain, was dedicated to the Virgin Mary. And the Chalice Well at Glastonbury, with its *chalybeate* (iron-infused) water that tastes like blood, is, precisely, the Holy Grail, or one aspect of it. The site was reputedly founded by Joseph of Arimathea, who, according to legend, brought the Grail containing Christ's blood to Glastonbury after the crucifixion; the monks would readily have identified the chalybeate water of the Chalice Well with the blood of the Savior, who is sometimes called a Fountain of Living Water.

The Chalice Well incarnates the lesser, feminine, psychic mysteries, the return to 'Adamic' state, to the human essence as God created it, the realization of the Earthly Paradise. The Tor on the hill directly above, sacred to St. Michael, set on St. Michael's Ley, is the Vertical Path, the *axis mundi*, a ray of the greater, masculine, Spiritual mysteries which lead to the transcendence of the human state, to Union with God. (First Lethe, then Eunoë; first the Earthly Paradise, then the *Paradiso* itself.) St. Michael in his icons is most often pictured carrying a lance— and so the mystery of the pairing of the Grail with the ever-bleeding Lance in the Grail romances is no mystery: the blood which mingles with the pure water of the Chalice Well ultimately comes from Above; the spear of Longinus piercing the heart of the crucified Christ, the lance of St. Michael, and the cross itself (like the Tor) are renditions of the *axis mundi*, the vertical path which unites the created universe with its unseen Source.

In 1906 a clairvoyant, Wesley Tudor Pole, had a vision that the Holy Grail was hidden in the Chalice Well at Glastonbury (as many sacred relics might well have been hidden by the monks when Henry VIII attacked and destroyed the Catholic monasteries). The Well was searched, and the searchers discovered therein a small blue glass dish, about six inches in diameter, with flakes of silver embedded in the glass. This is highly interesting in view of the fact that he Grail appears in the *Perceval* romance of Chretien de Troyes not as a stone or a cup, but as a shallow silver dish, somewhat like a patten, that is used to carry a consecrated host. And although it is described as a 'dish such as might be used to serve salmon or lampreys'—a large platter, in other words—this may be nothing but a bit of mis-direction to put relic thieves off the track: a dish that carries the Eucharist is thereby carrying *Ichthys*, Christ the Fish, the further implication being that the Fisher King in *Perceval* is actually in need of, and fishing for, Christ. And given that blue is the heraldic color of the Virgin Mary in the Western Christian tradition, and that silver is the Lunar metal and thus the pre-eminent symbol of archetypal femininity, we may conjecture that the dish found in the Well was considered to be an emblem of the Virgin. Gazing upon those flakes of silver embedded in dark blue glass, one is reminded of the starry midnight sky, particularly of the star-clouds of the Milky Way—and also of the star-embroidered cloak of the Virgin of Guadalupe, whose traditional image is the only true *icon* of the Western Church. Thus by all appearances the dish brought up out of the Chalice Well is emblematic of the Virgin Mary as Queen of Heaven.

In the Eastern Orthodox Christian icon of Our Lady of Glastonbury, the Virgin is overshadowed by a smaller figure of St. Michael, bearing the lance. The Virgin holds in her right hand the Glastonbury Thorn and in her left hand the Christ Child, himself carrying a globe of the starry heavens—which may in fact be symbolically equivalent to the Blue Bowl. In time and becoming, Christ Incarnate emerged from the matrix of the Virgin; in Eternity, Christ as God Himself carries her in the hollow of his in His hand, and gazes upon her forever, knowing her as the bearer of the constellations of all the eternal archetypes hidden in His secret Essence.

Esoterically speaking, the Holy Grail is the spiritual Heart, the inviolable center of the human soul, host to the Spirit of God in man, which is the Eye of the Heart—that reality called *Nous* by the Hesychasts and *Ruh* by the Sufis, and symbolized in the *Perceval* romance by the Host within the Grail. The same reality is concretely represented, in traditional Catholic iconography, by the image of the Holy Spirit in the form of a dove bringing a consecrated host down from heaven and holding it above a chalice as if ready to drop it in, as well as by the Catholic *monstrance*, a sacred vessel made of precious metal, often gold, and shaped like a sunburst or *mandala* set on a pedestal, with a circular 'eye' in the center of i—through which, under a glass cover, a consecrated host may be ritually contemplated. As the material Grail—if it ever existed—was the vessel that contained the flesh and blood of Christ, either carnally or under the species of bread and wine, so the Spiritual Grail contains both the outer Love and Knowledge of God (the bread), which is virtue, and the inner, esoteric Love and Knowledge of God (the wine), which is mystical Union. Whoever finds this Grail, and looks upon it with a constant and unwavering gaze, will be fed from it, healed of all his infirmities, and granted the boon of eternal life.

To a romantic and chivalric man, his human beloved is the earthly image of the Holy Grail, whose original form, now invisible due to the Fall of Man, resides in the Earthly Paradise, awaiting his return.

The End of Romance

Romance is *Maya*, creator and destroyer of the universe. There is the cynicism that wants to kill Romance in the name of the world; but 'What profit it a man if he gain the whole world, and lose his soul?' There is also the sobriety that kills it in the name of God: In the Kingdom of Heaven they 'neither marry nor are given in marriage.' But either way, toward the pit or toward the Most High, Romance is the Path.

The world kills Romance because the world is under judgment; the Kingdom of Heaven kills Romance by the Majesty of God—the divine power by which that world is judged.

On second thought, *no*—the Majesty cannot judge the world because it annihilates the world; it overturns the scales of judgment. The scales are Love; it's Love that judges the world—Love, more ruthless than Majesty, more merciful than Beauty itself.

In Dante's *Paradiso*, Beatrice disappears at one point; she is replaced by St. Bernard, to whom is attributed the saying, 'I love because I love.' This is love without romance, without the image of the Beloved; this is the moment when the page upon which is written 'Layla and Majnun' is torn in two, leaving only 'Majnun'. As Rabi'a said, 'when the Heart is fully awake, it needs no Friend.'

Only Love has the power—and the right—to lay romance in its tomb.

To My Wife

somnambulistic, I sweep the river—
—it carries the bones of the dead—
—the Roman centurion—wounded by
magic—become a serpent—his plume
and armor roll pulled by the current
along the lucid bottom, the wave-striped
cobbles—
all that I was—broken. all that I
called myself—the shards of my name
taken by the river. and, nameless,
my bone and my pith—my will
is a great cable—it will not
let you fall. beneath my ribs the
day is breaking—while you mourn
the passing of my shadow, confused
in the traces of the night—
for a moment you will miss me
while the day is taking us—my wife.
my true one. the reason
I have not died. the foundation
of my work—for a little while you
will not know the strength of my love—
you will see me taken by reveries—
by battles whose field is hidden
from you—while I hide myself
in indifference, or foolishness—
—but know that I have come to you
out of a distance farther than I can
remember, and not die. because I am
skilled in lamentation. because I
did not recoil from the pain I
owed to the wound I suffered
to those whom once I loved.
I have finished it. I have paid the price.
I am free. Now bind me.

PART TWO:
THE INWARD DIMENSION

by Jennifer Doane Upton

*'Whatever the world represses,
it becomes pregnant with.'*

High Romance
and the Spiritual Path

High romance is a quality of feeling that participates in the higher spiritual realities. It draws its life from the eternal, not the timely. High romance begins with human feeling, but far from stopping at the human level, this feeling goes on to higher spiritual worlds. Human love in some sense meets its death at the birth of divine love. But in another way, it lives on through that very death, as a symbol of that higher love. High romance involves passion and discipline. In a situation of either dry scholarship or sentimentality, there is no place for high romance. If high romance were present, the scholarship would be passionate, and the emotions disciplined. High romance is feeling oriented towards truth, toward knowledge. While we are contemplating the realities high romance points to, however, we must be humble enough to accept the human level which alone makes an understanding of the spiritual level possible to us.

⊕

The love of God is always secret. For most of us it is so secret that we are not even aware of it. All manifestations that appear around this love are false in a sense, and tend to misdirect us. To look for the love of God itself within manifest conditions is always to go astray. We spend our time in the world being attracted to this and repulsed by that, and all the while we are blind to this one secret love.

All stories about secret loves begin to reveal to us the love of God, even though in another sense they may be remote from this love.

⊕

We can miss the spirituality of a romantic story in two ways. One is to take it simply as a human love story, and not allow any realization of the spiritual dimension of human love to arise. The other is to treat it merely as an allegory, and try to cut out the human, the romantic level. Often those with some spiritual insight will relate to romantic material in just this way. If they see that the story is pointing toward higher realities, they believe they can ignore the human level and concentrate on the level of spiritual allegory alone. However, if one is not a romantic, one cannot reach a spiritual level of understanding by means of romantic literature.

In high romance, the spirit descends into and fills out the human level that is being expressed. Often, on account of the intensity of emotion this produces, we feel ashamed when we approach romantic material or states. All this loving of love, this having to do without love even as we love—it blisters our self-esteem. We reproach this state, as surely as the ladies of Egypt, in Jami's romance *Yusuf and Zuleika*, reproached Zuleika's love for Joseph. ('Yusuf' is the Arabic form of 'Joseph'; Zuleika is the name given in Islamic tradition to Potiphar's wife from the Book of Genesis.)

When we deny romantic states, we distort the very forms the Spirit is trying to ennoble. The Spirit hovers above us, with no way to reach our humanity. We have allowed it to be stranded.

⊕

In *Yusuf and Zuleika*, Yusuf is sold as a slave and taken into Egypt, and Zuleika, who buys him, falls in love with him. But Yusuf treats her with complete indifference. This is not because of an actual lack of love on his part, but because Yusuf deeply intuits that if their love were to be expressed in that time and in that state—Zuleika is a married woman—the fullness of that love would not be served. Since, however, his knowledge is intuitive, he cannot explain it to Zuleika. And even if this were possible, neither of them could explain it to the world.

Zulieka suffers, and word gets around about her love for Yusuf, and the humiliation it is bringing upon her. The ladies of Egypt protest that *they* would never fall in love with their slaves, and even if they did, they would certainly not be rejected by them; they are much too charming and attractive.

When Zuleika discovers that she's being talked about, she goes to the ladies and asks them: Have you ever seen Yusuf? And if not—would you like to? The ladies are surprised by this offer. But their curiosity draws them to accept it, and they have no reason to question their curiosity.

Zuleika invites them to a great banquet, and just as the fruit is being served, she brings Yusuf before them. When the ladies see him, they cut their own hands instead of the oranges they are holding. Love has come to them; but they, unlike Zuleika, have not taken a single step toward love. Thus, for the rest of their lives, they will be vulnerable to hysteria, insanity and emotional breakdowns. Pride, that enemy of love, has discovered that love is also *its* enemy, and so it can no longer give them its hideous protection.

⊕

An example of high romance from Western Europe can be found in Yeats' poem, 'The Three Bushes,' which was inspired by an incident from *Historia Mei Temporis* by the Abbe Michel de Bourdvielle; the following is my own rendition of the story:

A lady finds within herself deep feelings for a man to whom she cannot be married, and with whom she has no carnal relationship. Because of this, she feels the pain of her love's incompleteness, and this pain teaches her that if love does not naturally flower into wholeness, then it must in some way approximate wholeness—for her lover's sake if not for her own.

So that her lover might taste the love that her own soul has already tasted, she tells him that she will go to him at midnight, and their love will be consummated. But she agrees to do this only on condition that all will remain in darkness. She tells him that she cannot bear to see herself coming to him.

Nonetheless, the lady knows that her love for him cannot be consummated—not so much on account of propriety, but because her love is centered in the soul, and if it were to leave this soul-centeredness, it would be debased. She is unwilling to give her lover less than the highest love of which she is capable.

Still, the soul has its own generosity. The lady asks her maid, a woman untroubled by spiritual love, to go and take her place in the dark beside her lover. Midnight comes, and the maid willingly does what her lady has asked.

The lover blooms within a love whose wholeness he cannot comprehend. The lady finds her own happiness in watching him. However, when she sees her maid, the pain of love returns to her, because she knows that her love can only approximate wholeness. She will never be able to know that place to which her maid goes so easily.

This love-arrangement goes on for a full year; and during this period, the lover comes to see the sacred and the carnal as one. He remembers the first night his 'lady' came to him as if it were the only night. Whereas once he had sung songs, now he is speechless.

When he feels at last the completeness of this love, he decides to go out hunting. While on this trip, his horse puts its foot into a rabbit-hole, and throws him. He is killed. His lady sees all of this, and dies with him easily, for what is a death to the outer man is a marriage to the soul.

The maid, who has only the weight of her body to lift, lives a long time, and tends their graves. She plants a rosebush on each grave, and nurses them until they grow so large that they seem to come from a single root.

When she is dying, and the priest comes to her, she confesses everything, and asks to be buried beside the lover of her lady. As the priest listens, he hears how, after a lifetime of endurance, the body had finally tasted the love that the soul tastes easily. He cannot deny this body its own place. When she dies, the priest has her buried beside her lady's lover. He plants another rosebush on her grave, and tends those bushes so well that there comes a time when all three seem to spring from the same root.

$$\oplus$$

If we can't think, our ability to feel for what is true breaks down. If an imbalance exists within a person where he seems to be able to think and not feel, or feel and not think, that person's state can never be stable. Martin Lings, in his book *The Secret of Shakespeare*, speaks of Othello as a man who, through his love for Desdemona, can *love* the truth, but cannot *see* it. He has no spiritual vision. Since Othello cannot see the truth, he is completely vulnerable to Iago's lies. This recalls how Martin Lings, in his article 'The Signs of Times' from *The Sword of Gnosis*, speaks of the tendency of modern man to have deep feelings for his religion, but be unable to bring his intelligence to it, because everything he has been taught has forced him to secularize that intelligence. He is not allowed to *know* what it is that he feels for so deeply. His contemplative intelligence has not been born.

At the beginning of the play, Desdemona's father warns Othello that since he, the father, has been deceived by his daughter, she may well deceive Othello later on. The father feels betrayed because he perceives contradictions in Desdemona's behavior. When she shows no interest in the young men he introduces as suitors, he assumes that she isn't interested in marriage—but then she elopes with Othello, and seems to put her marriage to him before everything else. The father's impulse is to believe that Othello, through magical means, has cast a spell upon her. One might ask: What else can he believe? The father does not see Desdemona's true character, either before she elopes with Othello or afterwards.

His comment sows a seed of doubt in Othello that Iago is later able to play upon. The tragedy of the play lies in the fact that although Othello *feels* for Desdemona's character, he can no more *see* it than her father can. He knows that the accusation that *he* has practiced magic is false, but when he looks at the apparent contradictions in Desdemona's behavior that have made her father feel betrayed, he has no way to understand them. He cannot see how Maya has thrown a magical illusion over the whole situation—an illusion which Iago can exploit.

Othello, like the father, cannot see how Desdemona's lack of interest in eligible young men, far from implying a rejection of marriage itself, indicates a deep feeling for it. She feels the profundity of marriage within her soul; therefore, instead of accepting a marriage which will only make her happy on a social level, she waits for the one situation that will fulfill this profundity. When she meets Othello, she recognizes the opportunity for the fulfillment of the love her soul has prepared her for. This is why she can accept Othello immediately. All that Desdemona's father, however, and finally Othello himself, can see in this is unconventional behavior, and Othello fears that a woman who is capable of such behavior is likely to prove unfaithful. Maya has made her faithfulness in rejecting her false suitors and accepting without question her one true love look like flightiness and immaturity.

In the end, after Iago, through deception, has won Othello over to his way of seeing and caused him to kill Desdemona—which he cannot do without murdering his own truest feelings—his spiritual vision, according to Lings, is restored. After Desdemona's death, he sees her true character. Unfortunately, this insight comes too late to restore his loss on the terrestrial plane. Only through repentance can love and knowledge be reunited for him, though not on this earth. Without repentance, the true vision of who Desdemona is could never have come to Othello; for the sake of the salvation of his soul, his full human love must be restored to him, even though Desdemona no longer appears in this terrestrial world.

This vision causes him to give up his own life. That is, he gives up his present level of being, which contains everything he has known how to call life. As his vision leads him beyond himself, it brings back both his beloved wife and his deep love for her, and shows to him their eternal forms.

Divine Beauty: A Meditation

Beauty is one of the paths to spiritual Truth. Nothing compares with Beauty—that Beauty which attaches itself to the True, the Real, that is, and not that other beauty which participates almost completely in the world, and demands that we love this crass, habitual world, even if we have to swallow our truest feelings. That beauty breaks our hearts by putting up a wall between us and God, and finally tries to convince us that we can no longer reach God, and that God no longer wants us. How that beauty hates the other more beautiful Beauty, and does everything in its power to keep us from seeing it. It even puts out our eyes. But that other Beauty, the paradisiacal Beauty still comes to us, and when we are blind it penetrates the pores of our skin, for nothing in this world can deny us the vision of Paradise.

A Fable

I. Another Life

You brought evergreen boughs into my house, and put them around the cradle of our sick child. Then you knelt beside our child and prayed for it.

You died young, and I lived to be old. I longed for you throughout my long life.

⊕

You swore against the people of the unknown realms who had attacked our child.

'Who are these people?' I said. 'show them to me and I will burn them!'

You were astonished. 'There is so much your people don't know about,' you said.

⊕

You were a stranger. You came to my mother's house late at night, weary from traveling. You were kinder than the young men of my village, and more had happened to you in your brief lifetime. You had strange enemies.

I was afraid that you lived across the sea, and that when you returned to your homeland I would never be able to find you. Your people were a different people and spoke a different language. But you did not live far away from me. You were able to walk back to my village in a single day.

⊕

What love you had for me when we were first married! I still shiver when I think of you then. I thought your love for me disappeared just before you died. You dreamed so much about our child's enemies. In the daytime you talked about your father's ruin, and his failure in war. You had to live with his disgrace.

⊕

I am an old woman who is looking at another world: How can anything of beauty be left in me? Yet some men will look at me before they look at young girls. I wonder at beauty. After many years of blindness, the beauty of a young girl has come back to me.

I remember your face as if I had seen you yesterday. I expect you to be close to me. For days and days I've prayed to Our Lord to let me see you love me again. To be near you is to be near the fire.

II. Flood of Death

I will live in such a way as to be able to invite Death into my house as a guest. I won't fear any more all those emotional breakdowns (that are also a part of Death), wasted passions that rush through me, then leave me stranded in a sterile life, a life which I would not be able to rebuild because I would no longer have either the energy or the love.

So I will invite Death to eat with me and walk with me; he can even touch me if he likes. But since I will no longer gaze upon him, he will not be able to recognize me.

III. The People of Paradise

I found the People of Paradise in a place I hadn't expected them to be. The place was so simple that it could hardly be recognized, but their presence made it rich. They were able to put on their bodies like a garment, and when they did, they also put on Radiance.

When they spoke to me it was with such profundity of feeling that I knew I had been completely recognized. I knew that we were meant to be together, and that when they went away again, I would ask for no others.

IV. Mansions of Love

A Woman Writes a Letter to her Dead Husband:

I have to write to you now. I can't stand the constant banter; you're dead, they all say. They seem to have to come up to me and say 'you're dead' at just the time when it most hurts.

I have to write to you today because I know what they can't know. When I close my eyes to them and look into my soul, I know that it's not possible for you to be dead and me to be alive. If I am alive, you are alive. If we were together once, how could we not be together now?

A little while ago I went to visit my friends, and they talk about how easy it is to grow unloving toward a man. All the men they talk about are terrible. They leave their wives for other women, they're lazy, they drink, they lie, they beat their wives when the vegetables aren't cooked right. As my friends talk I recognize all this as having happened to me and I feel like them—but then the talking stops.

They bring out pictures of their men and spit on them and then something in me stops. I realize there is a wall between us, and I can go no further with these friendships.

I am closer to you now than I was then. My love for you never stopped. We were going along in our life together and then our life together went over a cliff, and you disappeared. Or is it I who disappeared.

I have changed so much I can hardly speak to any of my old friends. Every time I meet one of my friends I'm told, 'you're not what I expected.' Why do they want me to be something they expect, when I expect nothing of them?

I am growing older and everybody is saying nobody could possibly love her, her emotions are disastrous and her mind is beginning to become deranged. I go to my window in order to look out at them. They know so little about themselves. I turn away from that window quickly, because I have no calling to look for long upon those who have never seen the mansions of love.

V. Young Man

You are a man
whom I might meet again
as a stranger.
I have come so far
into this dream
that I am almost
talking with you again.
You are a young, dark man
who will not go back
into those hills you came out of.
you have not gone over
to the place of the dead;
you are calling to me
from the living.
You ask me to let my nights get longer,
to let the winter be,
for you were born in winter
and when we meet
it will be during winter.
Each time
I see you,
you are looking at me.
You do not take
my voice.
I would have called out to you
many years before this,
but to me
you gave no name.

VI. The Meeting

I, who have waited for you,
my husband,
am afraid of the place

you will bring me into.
I am backing away from you
now that you are here.
I heard your voice
near a small fire –
it has awakened my deadness.
O trees that are still unborn
stand away from me,
for I cannot touch your burning bark!

VII: Three Views of Paradise

One: Death and Paradise

Death has come to her
in the guise of a love that is
higher than her whole life.
She would have guarded against him,
but Death is a horseman that no one sees,
and now it is too late
to turn away from him,
for everywhere she looks she sees Death,
that dreadful messenger from Paradise.
Death stands here with half his being
already in Paradise,
and as he reaches toward her
with his horrible hand
he offers Paradise.
As she takes from him this gift,
she gives away all that is other than this gift.
She can never again see
the brokenness and incompleteness of her life
as anything other
than it is.
The illusory nature of the world
does not protect her.
Being undefended

on all sides,
she takes the joy of Paradise
not for its own sake,
but for the sake of a love
that is higher than Paradise.

Two: The Bridge

When she saw him she felt a peace that she had felt with no other. Who was he? Her own soul had never known such serenity. She had believed that she could experience this serenity in life, but she did not know that life could be 'here'. Where was 'here'? She had not died and she was not dreaming, but the world of her body had departed from her.

He had been standing on the bridge with his back to her. All his attention was absorbed in trying to see what lay beyond the bridge, but he couldn't see any of it. He turned around. When he saw her he said to himself, 'this is life. I never knew what life was like. If I had known this then, even when I had to risk life I would never have ungratefully possessed it. I know life "now".'

When was 'now'? Had he died? And if so, how long ago had his life ended? When the woman came up to him, he took her hand to greet her, and she said, 'I am so glad I have been able to come to you. This is what I really wanted.'

⊕

He no longer feared what lay beyond the bridge. He knew that whatever it was, it was not the pit of Hell. His guiding star was no longer a celestial body that would kill him if he came near to it, but a woman walking beside him.

⊕

She knew that he was with her even though she could find him nowhere in space or time. There is a space that is not the space our senses know, and there is a way of enduring that does not depend upon time.

⊕

In his life his soul had expanded into worldliness, not so much on account of an ambitious ego as because there was simply nothing in his surroundings to check it. Detachment is difficult.

When she came to him she came as an unknown grace, that very grace his life's expansion had blotted out. What could he feel for that soulless expansion now that he saw that it had only made him ignorant of mercy? Only now when he could no longer go back into life did he realize just what he had lost in being unable to recognize mercy. If he recognized this woman who came toward him now, it was because all during that expansion there was something in him that was not attached to it.

ç

He was between worlds. He had approached an idea, had tried to be an 'idealistic' man—and all along he had been unaware of how that idea had been approaching him. He had 'walked' into his death without being aware of what it was. Only now could he gaze upon its awesomeness.

⊕

Where was the bridge? It was in none of the places we call space, but it was for both of them more tangible than the roof of one's mouth. The unknown that they were both facing on the bridge was the same unknown; now it no longer mattered that they had come from different worlds. What were their worlds to them now? They were pieces of paper getting flimsier and flimsier as they departed from them. Their worlds had never been as real for either of them as this bridge was now.

Three: War's End

As soon as she recognized him, she realized that she had lost him. After her long search, all that remained to her was a loss. She thought that if she went toward him she would find his grave, but instead she came upon the brutal place of war—the war within her soul that had enabled her to find him.

She wanted Paradise. She wanted to find him there. But Paradise has its own awesomeness. The deep love of Paradise is as rigorous as war. That love reaches down into our lower world and absorbs its places of pain, in order to heal them.

When she looked again she found no war. He had been in those places of pain, and there had been no other.

Now he was in repose. Great peace and great love were opening into God.

Reflections
on St. Xenia
of St. Petersburg

St. Xenia is described in the Eastern Orthodox liturgy for her feast on January 24 as one who has broken with the vanity and the illusory character of this world. One can't help but ask: What is this illusion, this world which she feels it is so imperative to break with?

The narrative of her life is simple. As a young woman she marries a professional entertainer connected with the military. He lives an artistic and dissipated life which eventually ends in sudden death without the last rites of the church.

When he dies everything changes for Xenia. She gives away the home they had kept together and begins to travel as a pilgrim. The world can never again be her home. Now if she is to have a home, even in her thoughts, she must intuit that true homeland which is always strangely present to those whose longing for it is real. Eventually she returns to St. Petersburg— perhaps, however, not until her knowledge of that true homeland, which is not other than Paradise, has become so complete that she can easily disregard what the world calls real and present, all of which is so easily corrupted by time.

When she returned to St. Petersburg, in no way was she trying to return *home*. Everything had changed. Her relationship to her native city was precarious. She dressed in rags and remained without shelter in the Russian winter, miraculously protected from the cold by her faith in God. She was homeless. Sometimes people threw mud and stones at her; at other times they came to her with reverence because she could see into their futures as they could not. Perhaps the same people who threw stones at her would later be among the ones who came to her, seeking the truth about themselves. Some of those people may even have reflected how, if the part of the soul which revered her found truth, then that part which had reviled her must be false.

She wore her dead husband's military uniform. She went even further, and demanded that people call her by her husband's name, Andrei. It was as if she were saying 'Every day you tell yourself that you see Xenia walking about your streets, the same one who traveled to the far corners of her world seeking truth. You see Xenia continuously giving away clothes which had been given to her, becoming more and more of a saint every day and thereby gaining your respect. But beware! You only see what appears; you do not see the truth of things.'

'It is Andrei you see. It is he who goes about the streets of St. Petersburg giving away the alms others have given him. It is Andrei who in the nighttime climbs the edifice of the church being built, carrying bricks in order to help the workman in their work. In truth it is Andrei whom you see becoming a saint. As for Xenia, she is not here. It has been a long time since there has been anything of Xenia which you could see. When you look toward her you do not find her. Therefore it is a mercy that, when you look to Xenia, instead of seeing a nobody, you see Andrei. You are allowed to see him because it is he who is becoming a saint, not Xenia. It is Andrei who in giving away all his material possessions gives himself away. It is Andrei who, in telling you your futures, is showing you that the love of God goes deeper than you ever knew. As for Xenia, she allows you to forget her as completely as she has forgotten herself.' When she visited people's houses, she would often say, 'Here is all of me!'. She says this because nothing is left of her that could exclude or contradict this particular 'here'. Because she has no home, she is at home everywhere. Because she has no self, nothing in her contradicts the self she presents to others as their guest.

Sometimes Xenia, in calling herself Andrei, is associated with St. Andrew, the fool-for-Christ, who in Constantinople had a vision of the Mother of God lifting her veil. This is the vision upon which the feast of the Protecting Veil, on the 1st of October, is based. One can imagine the veil of the Mother of God being so broad that it embraces Xenia's veil. Xenia lifted her own veil long enough to show us a mercy which we cannot know in an ordinary way. When, however, we grasp the bit of that mercy which we *are* able to see, and go in search of Xenia as an 'ordinary' person, then that Veil falls over us, and separates us even from the love that we used to know.

$$\oplus$$

Commentary

In some ways Andrei is a type of that aspect of God which is manifested, while Xenia represents the aspect which is never manifested, even though she remains a person. Andrei has a name, whereas Xenia—whose name means 'stranger'—denies others permission to give her a name, other than Andrei. However, in another way, it is Xenia who is the living person, whereas Andrew is now nothing but a jacket that she wears. All this is an oblique way of talking about what of God can be revealed, and what of Him must remain hidden. Also, it shows how, at times, the two aspects, the manifest and the unmanifest, mysteriously change places.

On Love and Wisdom

God is Love, but He is also Wisdom. And since all duality has its roots in the illusory world, these divine aspects are not two, but One. Sometimes we name this One 'Wisdom'; sometimes we name it 'Love'.

Our mother religion has been Christianity and this tradition, in its attempt to distance itself from dangerous heresies, has often put a veil over true gnosis, that is, Divine Wisdom. Gnosis, of course, has always been in the heart of our religion. In its own way it has been the light which shines in the darkness. For a long time, however, that gnosis has been rarely spoken of.

Divine Wisdom is the pearl of great price which we cannot overvalue. We who value Wisdom are wrong, however, to look upon her as a proud secret, and Love as an intruder. After all, it is Divine Love who is Wisdom's Bridegroom, and not we ourselves.

We do not recognize Love because of the mysterious shapes in which it appears to us. Divine Knowledge is the crown of Being and its glory is self-evident. Love, however, leaves its footprints in the most unlikely aspects of our soul—as Beatrice, in Dante's *Inferno*, left her footprint in deepest Hell. Sometimes because of Love we, like Dante, must look upon Hell for the first time. Without the love and intercession of Beatrice, Dante would never have seen the face of Hell. But without the vision of Hell, there would have been no way for him to travel on, through Purgatory, to Paradise.

When Love draws near to us we fear chaos, because Divine Love can stare chaos in the face in a way that Divine Knowledge is never asked to do. This is why we have the tradition that Christ harrowed Hell. When we see Christ descending into Hell so that our own inner hells may be transformed, we experience an event of unutterable Beauty—a Beauty which would bind the faculties of the soul, were not Divine Love there to set us free.

We understand that since the gnostic knows the world through Divine Wisdom, he is able to see the Beauty therein, especially in the realm of nature. But Divine Beauty is inseparable from Love. How can we then, having once seen this otherworldly Beauty, denigrate Love in any form? Hasn't the lover at least begun to *know* that which he loves?

Some who value Divine Wisdom have seemed to say, in the name of Divine Beauty, that love of neighbor is somehow less than love of virgin nature. Other human beings, however—our brothers and sisters in the human state—are the crown of nature in this visible world. The last revenge of Hell against *gnosis* would be to present us with a vision of Beauty without Love.

But those who deny Wisdom in the name of Love, because they don't want to be thought of as 'Gnostics', are equally in error. They will end by betraying Love, because without insight there is no Truth, and Love cannot be based on a lie.

The Stones of Men

I have looked for you in the faces
of all those people who turn backward
like the sun turning toward death
for fear of you, whom they might see.

I have asked for your whereabouts everywhere,
and every place upon this earth has been revealed to me.
I cannot hold
all I see.

Now, if I think about you at all, I hide it.
I hold my voice back in the market place
to keep from talking about you.

Today I have not met a single person who is not heartless.
I have not met a single person who does not believe
that I am already staying with you
whom I am searching for.

These are the stones given to all men and women.
Not one of us can live a single day
sitting upon this pile of stones.

The Mountains

I have been told that the mountains
would help me,
And yet in the mountains
I find no peace.
When I look toward them,
I still do not see them all.

The mountains are all people
before the mouth of their heart opens,
and today all the mountains
have crushed in upon my marriage-grave.

Today I can dream no longer.
The landscape I am walking through
is neither my dream nor yours --
and I,
who now know the faces
of so many men and women
no longer know where the place is
in which I last lay down.

The Call

He took his arm away from the window
and she believed he had reached
for her.
Then he died,
and she went out to search for his body,
but oh the black, black earth
was never him.

'O you clouds, you atmosphere that makes rain,
now hear human speech for the first time.
Bring back to me his living body,
and wash the dust out of his throat
that he may speak.

Tear him from the arms
of all those who have despaired
of true love,
and let him come to me, alone
as I am alone
in this night—

for he has called to me, and this time
I have not turned back.'

The Massacre

Sometimes I feel that the dead
are mourning for us.
They approach when we can't see them
They talk to us when we can't hear them
and no matter how much they try to touch us,
we always forget the knowledge
that when we lost them
we also lost ourselves.

I feel within my nightmares
the cruelty they experience when they love us—
Wanting to speak to us
means wanting to have the very bodies
it has just become impossible for them to have.
We always look upon them as souls
and we say we love them with our soul—
Our bodies no longer know how to love them.

And in their own way they are cruel to us.
By the time we remember
recently forgotten names
they have already changed
and left us with the love that was rightfully ours
from the beginning.
It is only we, whose knowledge comes from our
*   bodily lives*
who can turn their cruelty
back into tenderness.

The Meeting with God

I, who do not know my own soul's name
have already seen her,
disguised as the shadow of a river,
saying to me:

'Cry as much as you can
for you cannot live another day
without meeting God.
Your heart cannot be broken more.'

When I came back into the world
all those of the world made me forget you,
saying that I'd loved you more
than anyone could love God;
God would punish me, they all said,
by making me love even more.
How can I pretend not to know you
when I have loved you since
before the day I was born?
You are among a new people.
And my soul has come here
to help me find you.

'Give up the last thing you could own,'
*   she says,*
'Take the last bite of food out of
*   your mouth.*
Give up this life.'

The Return

You, who I thought
was so far away—
you, are now standing
in my door.

Look at me—
since you have gone away
I too have become life and death.
The dead child I have
put into the earth,
and the living one I have
hidden away.

The dishes I meant
to set the table with
when you came back
are cracked now,
and I can no longer buy
electricity—
but come, and eat
upon this bright tablecloth,
for toward evening
the sun makes
this whole house glow.

And always, toward evening
I see you
as I saw you five years ago,
about to leave
and about to come back to me
in a single step.
We had just buried the dead child,
and the living child
which you never knew
I am still hiding.

The Rain in the Desert

'This is my nightmare,'
she said to the strange one,
    the beloved—
'Watch it come upon me
like the rain which comes into
the desert and floods it.
How can I, who have no home
promise to give one
    to you,
I who am walking
    to where the roads change?'

She, who had been too asleep
to remember the strange one,
the beloved
and what he said
now wakes up saying:

    'This is a day
which comes early in my life.'

Speech and Silence

If language is going to take us back to God, it will take us through silence.

Language is human, but it has a divine origin. Human beings cannot create a true language by their own efforts.

Speech is manifestation. We can only speak about what can be said, about what has already descended into the manifest world—but what happens when what can be said marries what cannot be said?

A certain man who made things so clear to us through words always had with him his invisible wife, whom he never talked about because he knew how much we dreaded even the thought of seeing her. He talked to us in perfect speech, then went away—and we began to long for what we could not see. We clung to his perfect speech. We memorized it. We even thought we could make that speech more perfect.

Who were we, who every day went out looking for other than what we saw? Who were we to imagine that our speech even remotely resembled the perfect speech of this man?

We didn't know that the speech of this man had enthralled us with all the invisible ways we dreaded. We blamed his wife for our dread. When our backbiting got to be too much even for her invisible ways, she would get up and leave the table, and then we would blame her even more—talking behind her back, and complaining that she revealed too many secrets.

And since we could not recognize our own dread, it used us to create its own dreadful world. It is into this very world of dread that the man with his perfect speech came. It was that very speech which would help us overcome that dread.

We, who have overcome that dread, have become silent.

The Zahir is the shadow of the Rose
And the rending of the veil.

Fariduddin Attar

www.ingramcontent.com/pod-product-compliance
Lightning Source LLC
Chambersburg PA
CBHW031203270326
41931CB00006B/382